Romanticism in Focus

by
Lucien Jenkins

Also available from Rhinegold Publishing:
Modernism in Focus
Baroque Music in Focus
Madonna in Focus
Who's Next in Focus
Batman in Focus
Goldfinger in Focus

Rhinegold Study Guides
Students' Guides to GCSE, AS and A2 Music for the AQA, Edexcel and OCR Specifications
Listening Tests for GCSE, AS and A2 Music for the AQA, Edexcel and OCR Specifications

A Student's Guide to GCSE Music for the WJEC Specification
A Student's Guide to Music Technology for the Edexcel AS and A2 Specification
Listening Tests for Students: Edexcel AS and A2 Music Technology Specification

A Student's Guide to AS Classical Civilisation for the AQA Specification

Students' Guides to AS and A2 Drama and Theatre Studies for the AQA and Edexcel Specifications

Students' Guides to AS and A2 Performance Studies for the OCR Specification
Students' Guides to AS and A2 Religious Studies for the AQA, Edexcel and OCR Specifications

Rhinegold Publishing also publishes Classical Music, Classroom Music, Early Music Today, Music Teacher, Opera Now, Piano, The Singer, Teaching Drama, British and International Music Yearbook, British Performing Arts Yearbook, Rhinegold Guide to Music Education, Rhinegold Dictionary of Music in Sound.

First published 2007 in Great Britain by
Rhinegold Publishing Ltd
241 Shaftesbury Avenue
London WC2H 8TF
Telephone: 020 7333 1720
Fax: 020 7333 1765
www.rhinegold.co.uk

Romanticism in Focus
British Library Cataloguing in Publication Data.
A catalogue record for this book is available from the British Library.
ISBN: 978-1-906178-14-7
Printed in Great Britain by Thanet Press

Contents

The author

Lucien Jenkins is the author of *Laying out the Body* (poems from Seren Books) and *Modernism in Focus* (Rhinegold 2007), and co-author of the *Classical Music Encyclopedia* (Collins 2000). His edition of the *Collected Poems* of George Eliot was praised by Gillian Beer in the *Times Literary Supplement*. His editions of *The Necromancer* by Peter Teuthold and *The Midnight Bell* by Francis Lathom (two of the gothic novels cited in Austen's *Northanger Abbey*) were welcomed by *The Year's Work in English Studies*. His book with CDs for Naxos *Discover Early Music* was called a 'clear, well-informed introduction... In dealing with more complex forms, Jenkins excels. He lays out just enough information to make the general listener aware of the kinds of things that are happening without going into intimidating detail' (*All Music Guide*). He is also the editor of the *Rhinegold Dictionary of Music in Sound* (Rhinegold Publishing 2001) and *The Illustrated Musical Instruments Handbook* (Flame Tree 2006).

He studied for his BA at Cambridge University, and for his MA and his PhD at London University. He has taught for Ruskin College, Oxford, the Open University and Bristol University's lifelong learning department. He is a former member of the board of the Poetry Society, and has worked as a reviewer, critic and journalist for history, literature, dance, music and the visual arts. He was a member of the Qualifications and Curriculum Authority's Music Development Group (helping rewrite the music content of the National Curriculum), and has been a judge in the Classic FM Music Teacher of the Year since its inception. He is the former editor of *Music Teacher,* and the founder of *Early Music Today, Classroom Music* and *Teaching Drama.*

The Editors

Sophie Buchan, Rose Vickridge, Rosamund Spinnler and Chris Elcombe.

Acknowledgments

The author and publisher wish to remember W. R. Dalzell and to thank Hugh Benham and John Walker for their help in the preparation of this book. Thanks also to Milos Luzanin, the Trustees of the British Museum and Elke Walford of the Hamburger Kunsthalle for their kind permission to reproduce the images on the cover.

Preface

Romanticism is the most successful arts movement in modern history. Dominating the 19th century, its influence continued to be felt right through the 20th century and into the present day. Where Modernist works of the early 20th century startled, and continue to startle readers and audiences alike, Romantic poetry, fiction, art, architecture and music won over sometimes initially suspicious contemporaries, and their grip on our sense of the arts today is unweakened. One might even suggest that where Modernist (in the widest sense) works are now making their way into the mainstream, it is perhaps because they allow marketing departments to adopt a Romantic presentation. Many people exclusively read and listen to the fiction and music of Romanticism, whether Tchaikovsky, Verdi and Puccini, or Dickens, Brontë and Tolstoy. Others whose interests are broader unwittingly judge everything against the Romantic repertory.

> Examples of soon-to-be canonic Modernist works include Schoenberg's *Verklärte Nacht*, Berg's violin concerto and Messiaen's *Quatuour pour le fin du temps*.

In the field of popular entertainment, fiction, music and films continue to be built according to Romantic aesthetic principles and to express a Romantic code of values. Thumb through consumer magazines of every kind and you will find they combine models, houses and lifestyle stories to encode a Romantic inheritance. Indeed, an entire strand of entertainment in fiction and films has taken over the name of 'romance' for itself.

When writers and painters gathered in the late 19th century, they congregated in Paris, the city of Hugo, Baudelaire and Berlioz. Even as Modernism was seizing the intellectual agenda, such was the power of Romanticism over our sense of the arts that Paris continued to be the place to which composers and writers flocked. George Orwell, in an essay on Henry Miller dating from 1940 ('Inside the Whale'), invites us to laugh at the perceived excesses of the Bohemian lifestyle; he is clearly confident that all his Anglophone readers will recognise the characters and costume of the topic, even if only at third hand. Indeed, such images of Parisian Bohemians are so iconic and universally recognisable, they are even to be found in a scene from Disney's 1970 cartoon *The Aristocats*.

> The opera *La bohème* takes its title and plot from an 1851 Romantic work of fiction, Henri Murger's *Scènes de la vie de Bohème*.

Biographical books and films that deal with artists of pre-Romantic generations frequently reconstruct their subjects according to the biography we have been taught to expect by Romanticism. It would appear we have become convinced that there is no other way of being an artist: no biography is complete without the neglect, the struggle with anguish or mental illness, the loneliness, the loyalty of a perceptive friend or patron, the posthumous recognition, and so on. Our sense of what a creative artist should be has been so decisively affected by Romanticism that pop and cinema stars continue to ape a code of behaviour enacted by de Nerval and codified by Baudelaire in the first half of the 19th century. Conservative parties still find it difficult to line up pop stars for celebrity endorsements during election campaigns: the memory that Beethoven supported the French Revolution and Wagner the 1848 uprising clearly remains fresh.

Perhaps the paucity of biopics of Bach stems from the utter impossibility of even Hollywood's creativity to shoehorn him into their glass slipper of preconceptions. Don't hold your breath for a Shaffer play called *Sebastian* or a Stoppard screenplay called *Bach in Love*.

The declaration that Margaret Thatcher was 'the first Spice Girl' was hastily hushed up by promoters who understood cultural history, and the century-long animosity between the creative artist and conservative forces.

Yet Romanticism is certainly not famous for inventing new art forms. The genres by which we know it best – the concerto, the landscape, the Lied, the novel, the ode, the opera, the sonata, the sonnet, the string quartet, the symphony – generally have Baroque origins and have been defined by the Classical period. Certainly, Romanticism took many of them into new worlds, but Romantic artists did not have to invent or even reinvent them. If one makes a study of early 19th-century painting, writing and composing, and where possible reads the letters or table-talk of the artists themselves, one is more struck by their respect for and study of their artistic forefathers – most notably Clementi, Dussek, Handel, Haydn; Caravaggio, Claude, David, Titian; Grey, Richardson, Thompson, Young – than by any intention to overthrow tradition.

Examining influences, sources and transitional works is interesting work. I regret the absence here of *Sturm und Drang*, Anne Elliot noticing the landscape in *Persuasion* and Ann Radcliffe, who was read by several Romantic poets, including Keats.

So what was it about Romanticism that allowed it to take Europe and then the world by storm in this way, enduringly affecting our taste and judgement in the arts and in life more widely?

1
The historical context

The liberty debate

The **American Revolution** of 1776 made a profound impact on the European psyche. It demonstrated:

- The overthrow of a monarch
- The overthrow of an imperial power by a colony
- The birth of a nation
- The self-determination of a people.

The appeal of this upheaval to those who wanted freedom for occupied countries or peoples seeking self-determination was enormous. But the implications were also felt closer to home, especially among the European radicals who wanted to bring about the fall of the *Ancien Régime* of absolute monarchs. The possibility of political change in a European context was realised over a decade later, in the form of the **French Revolution** (1789), which reinforced the atmosphere of change and created a sense that human beings could do two extraordinary things:

- Challenge kings
- Challenge God.

This may appear an over-ambitious set of conclusions to have reached. However, the *Ancien Régime*'s apologists had preached that kings ruled because God had placed them on their thrones, and the result was that the revolutionary view was to some extent that mankind need not be dictated to by God. Indeed it is difficult to underestimate the extent to which the conservative (anti-change) position had interlinked all aspects of economy, society, culture and religion. Therefore the radical attack, by necessity, fell on every flank.

Mary Shelley's depiction of Dr Frankenstein's experiments on dead bodies formed a critique of contemporary advances in science's understanding of how the human body works. *Frankenstein* (1818) shows a man whose scientific endeavours go beyond the ambition to cure diseases. He seizes the divine initiative and, while not creating life, at least conquers death – something that the churches had proclaimed as the purpose and achievement of Christ alone.

In the creature's subsequent rebellion against his creator, Romantic mankind's rebellion against God takes another, somewhat paradoxical form.

> This double, conflicting, rebellion is a theme which shall be returned to shortly.

Two leading contributors to the debate on liberty were **Thomas Paine** (1737–1809) and **Edmund Burke** (1729–1797). Paine declared that 'An Englishman is not free of his own country', comparing England unfavourably with both France and America. But Burke was equally principled and, according to some readings, equally radical. He favoured reconciliation with the revolted American colonists, greater independence from royal direction for the House of Commons and the emancipation of his native Ireland.

Burke was attacked for his supposed opposition to freedom, but his case was that Britain possessed a history of freedom, which France did not. He also believed that the revolution would lead to less, not more, freedom, the triumph of partisan self-interest and ultimately a military coup. These assertions proved impressively true and Burke's reputation was considerably salvaged by his prescience. The case he set out in *Reflections on the Revolution in France* (published in 1790, only a year after the Revolution happened) was not against freedom but for the rule of law, a very Classical position, as later chapters will make clear.

The aftermath of the French and American revolutions revealed that in acting on your own desire for liberty, you unwittingly compromise someone else's. An example of this unfolded on the island of Hispaniola, where the son of a Dahomey chief, **Toussaint L'Ouverture**, was leading a successful insurrection of black slaves. Island society was a complex mix of white French colonists, black slaves and mulattos (people of mixed descent), each group harbouring its own political ambitions. Toussaint believed in the ideals of the French Revolution and was convinced that the rights of man, not independence, should be his people's goal. The mulattos did not identify with the ambition of the black slaves. The white French were concerned to secure their own position at the expense of anyone who stood in their way, all the while feeling the effects of the shifts in power back in France. Haiti became independent, but Toussaint died in prison, immortalised by a sonnet in his praise by Wordsworth.

> Wordsworth himself was a visitor to revolutionary France and had an affair and fathered a child while sightseeing. See *Wordsworth: A Life*, Stephen Gill; Gill has also edited a *Selected Poems* for Penguin.

The year 1830 saw another revolution in France, with King Louis Philippe acceding to the throne, as well as a key moment in the creation of modern Belgium (see page 10). In Britain, the following year played host to the Merthyr Rising, with what felt to Merthyr Tydfil's participants like the beginnings of a revolution; troops were sent in by steamship to put it down. The waving of tricolours at the opening of the Liverpool and Manchester Railway was a reminder that the legend, if not the facts, of the French Revolution remained fresh in radical memory.

Napoleon

The next radical date is **1848**, a year which saw the election of President Louis Napoleon, later to be crowned Emperor Napoleon III, as well as radical revolutions and nationalist uprisings in several countries. Meanwhile, the 35-year-old Wagner was engaged in pamphleteering in Saxony and, following the collapse of the radical programme, was forced to flee. In the same year, Marx was expelled

> 1848 was also the year in which Dickens published *Dombey and Son* and Elizabeth Gaskell *Mary Barton*; Charlotte Brontë's *Shirley* came out the following year.

from Cologne (for the second time) for editing a left-wing newspaper.

Oddly enough, Jean-François **Napoleon** Buonaparte's family hadn't actually wanted to be French. His homeland of Corsica had only become part of France the year before he was born and his family's politics were separatist: they supported the Corsican nationalist Pasquali Paoli.

Had the dice of history rolled differently, Napoleon might have found himself a Corsican ambassador, jurist or general. In fact, the island's union with France in 1768 was followed by the 1792 Revolution which drove much of the aristocracy out of the country and opened up

> Commentators have pointed to the fact that some other ambitious young generals who might have been rivals for supreme power had coincidentally died ahead of Napoleon's return to Paris.

previously undreamt of career possibilities for men of ambition. In addition, the army both grew in size and removed foreigners from its ranks. This was to be a large, professional, all-French conscript army, defending the Revolution – and then exporting it under Napoleon to all of Europe, from Spain to Russia, and Sweden to Sicily. The fact that Edmund Burke was able to predict a military coup as early as 1790 in his *Reflections on the Revolution in France*, with such accuracy, indicates that Napoleon's rise was a conspiracy of circumstances and character.

A view from Germany

German patriotism was every bit as complex as French at this time, although for different reasons. France was a cultural concept undergoing redefinition, since the intermittent social upheavals meant that loyalty to 'France' was confused with loyalty to one or other political programme and combatant group within the country. Germany had yet to exist except as a cultural entity. Through much of the Romantic period it was a patchwork quilt of countries of varying size and varying degrees of independence. Before the rise of military nationalism leading to the Franco-Prussian War and the declaration of the Second Empire in the Hall of Mirrors at Versailles, a cultural nationalism was expressed through the arts by drawing attention to unifying national works of human achievement or natural beauty such as the Rhine or Cologne Cathedral.

In a sense, however, the declaration of the Second Empire was in itself a calculatedly Romantic event, designed to appeal to the sense of history inadvertently shared by the Prussian Junkers and the German-speaking intellectuals who tended to be of a more liberal political creed. Anton von Werner's painting that recorded the event, like that of the coronation of Napoleon I by Jacques-Louis David, is an iconic work that rewards further study. Similarly, its progeny, the Treaty of Versailles (the subject of yet another set-piece painting), contained a series of announcements of nationhood in the aftermath of the First World War and under the patronage of Woodrow Wilson, convinced – as Americans tend to be – of the importance of national self-determination.

> An image search on the internet will quickly find these paintings.

Nationalism

Belgium and **Poland** are two sides of the 19th-century nationalist coin. In the case of Poland, the state did not exist from 1795 to 1918. As a result, it is for many the definitive Romantic cause, since its quest for self-determination spans the entire century in question, and involves Napoleon, as he recreated a Polish state, only for it to be partitioned again at the Congress of Vienna in 1815.

Belgium's history is obscured by changes of name and owner. As part of Burgundy, it had been home to some of the greatest cultural achievements of its times, giving us the Van Eycks, Van Dyck and Rubens, and in the figure of Orlandus Lassus, a composer known to his contemporaries as the Michelangelo of music. Through Habsburg marriages it found itself administered by Spain and then by Austria.

> Lassus is the Latin form of his name. A well-travelled Renaissance composer, his name exists also in French and Italian versions.

The Romantic movement picked up on this political indeterminacy: the plot to Verdi's opera *Don Carlos* (1867) is framed by the region's political situation, as is Goethe's play *Egmont* (1787), and the Beethoven overture of the same name (1809). Beethoven responded to the tale less because of its nationalist history (the creation of the Dutch state) than because of its heroic and libertarian programme, which we could interpret as 'Napoleon without the military coup'. Verdi, a later Romantic, was writing from Italy, a country which was equally trying to find its identity, and did so in a process known the *Risorgimento*. Once again, the nationalist struggle was closely linked with concepts of liberty and socialism: Cavour may have created the Italian state through shrewd political ability and ambitions for the Piedmontese crown, but Garibaldi did so on a socialist programme.

Belgium created a national identity in part by appeal to its medieval history in the shape of a Bill of Rights dating from 1356. This was the equivalent of England's Magna Carta, a document often cited at the time to justify the Chartist movement. This movement sought both to advance the rights of man and to restore liberties perceived as lost, and is mentioned in several British Romantic 'industrial' novels such as Eliot's *Felix Holt*.

All of these nationalist developments are recorded in Romantic works of art in various media. A web search will take you to Gustav Wappers' set piece *Episode During the Belgium Revolution of 1830*. Adam Mickiewicz is the leading exponent of Polish Romantic poetry and the subject of a suitably meditative yet brooding portrait by Walenty Wánkowicz. Chopin, abroad during the 1830 uprising, was the first composer to introduce the Mazurka, a lively folk dance in triple meter, and the Polonaise, a slower dance in $\frac{3}{4}$ time, to western art music. These forms were, to Chopin, his link to the lost homeland, a way of creating a Poland in culture that had ceased to exist in politics and geography. Beethoven marked the concluding Largo of his op 56 triple concerto 'alla polacca' (1804), while Tchaikovsky includes six Mazurkas in *Swan Lake* (1877). Tolstoy's *Anna Karenina* (also 1877) also includes a Mazurka in a ball.

> Note that Tchaikovsky was not the only Russian composer to exploit the Mazurka.

However, when we consider that Russia owned most of (east) Poland at this time, while Austria and Prussia shared the rest, the question arises: were Beethoven and the Russians assuming cultural ownership, expressing sympathy with Polish captivity, or just enjoying the sound of a folk dance at a time when such things were in fashion?

Music did not have to be folk-based to express national aspiration – it didn't even have to be local. In Belgium, a performance of Auber's opera *La Muette de Portici* took Brussels by storm, as it seemed to sum up the country's own struggle. In Italy, Giuseppe Verdi's very name became a political slogan, in part because of his cultural achievements and political views, but in part simply because his name was an acronym for 'Vittorio Emanuele, Re D'Italia', and thus for unification.

> Wagner once claimed that Auber's work was the pinnacle of French operatic achievement, 'a national work of the sort that each nation has only one of at the most'. See *Cambridge Companion to Grand Opera* ed. David Charlton, CUP 2003, pages 179–180.

Britain in flux

British churches felt the effect of Romanticism, moving from the comfortable rationality depicted in 18th-century fiction (which combined idleness and a lack of theology with welfare work) to an age of evangelicalism and missionary work prefigured by Methodism. The Oxford Movement was an affiliation of High Church Anglicans who sought to demonstrate that the Church of England was a direct descendant of the Christian church established by the Apostles. As a result, a significant number of Catholic practices were introduced into worship. It was a quintessentially Romantic development in church life, just as Unitarianism had been the guiding light of the closing years of the Age of Reason. However, the Romantic world had a wilder, more outward-looking spirit, one which sent David Livingstone preaching the gospel in southern Africa as surely as it sent Arthur Rimbaud to sell guns in the north (and Charles Baudelaire into the arms of an African mistress).

This was still an age of change in agricultural practice and the changes fired a desire for further **enclosure acts**. There had been considerable distress concerning enclosures during the Tudor period, but the 18th and early 19th century saw vastly more land enclosed. The autobiography of Thomas Bewick and the poetry of John Clare both point to socio-economic loss, but both reflect on aesthetic losses as well. There was a powerful sense among a range of artists that something had happened and was happening in society which went against the true nature of human beings.

> The amount of enclosed land in question during the 16th century was tiny, but the upheaval generated was a reflection of the relative inflexibility of the (essentially late-Medieval) economy.

Silas Marner's (see page 37) laconic description of Raveloe tells of a rural society supported by a war economy, and making no attempt to progress or improve. Other novels, however, tell of the rise of radical politics among the industrial working classes. A prime example

> See 'England 1782–1832' by Colin Brooks, in *The Romantics* ed. Stephen Prickett, Methuen 1981, page 47.

of this is the depiction of trade unionism in Dickens' *Hard Times*. This was indicative of Britain's ongoing **industrialisation** and subsequent internal migration from the countryside to industrial towns, which resulted in Birmingham, Leicester and Sheffield seeing their populations double in the first quarter of the 19th century. Little wonder that when Silas Marner revisits the town of his youth he finds Lantern Yard not only gone but entirely forgotten by the locals. The built environment was changing at a frightening pace.

The belief that it was possible to find one specific point in history where everything went wrong became widespread in a secular version of lapsarian theology. Contemporary analyses of human vice, building on an Augustan poetic conceit, reached the conclusion that the town was where all human wickedness was to be found. The implications of this belief are to be found in poets as different as Wordsworth and Alphonse de Lamartine, who both reflect on the sanctity of the landscape and sublimity of the rural life, while Blake and Baudelaire focus on London and Paris respectively. Within this rural/urban dialectic, all these poets are engaged in negotiations with, or attacks upon, a conservative Christian analysis of good and evil.

In **Jane Austen**, the characterisation of Mrs Elton (*Emma*) is inherently a criticism of the new mercantile class and their town values. Coming from Bristol (and inevitably rather touchy on the subject of the slave trade), Augusta Elton quite misjudges her rural neighbours and patronises even Mr Knightley. Her declaration that she detests upstarts and her hostility to Maple Grove's new neighbours, the Tupmans – she declares that 'One has not great hopes of Birmingham' – show her clearly trying to distinguish herself from those still close to trade. The Tupmans (and indeed her own family) are part of the same insurgence of new money and new political confidence as is to be found in *Bleak House*'s Rouncewell, a man not afraid to meet Sir Leicester Dedlock, despite being his servant's son.

> The name Maple Grove is worth analysing in itself, as it indicates fashion in tree-planting and is probably supposed to be contrasted with 'oak' and 'forest'. Several English romantic novelists retain the Medieval habit of naming characters or places to indicate their moral status, a practice fed into the English novel by John Bunyan.

Yet do Austen and Dickens believe that all was well before industrialisation? The briefest glance at Sir Leicester, Lady Caroline de Bourgh (*Pride and Prejudice*) or the Bertram sisters (*Mansfield Park*) is enough to show that they are as cool about deference, patronage and old, landed wealth as they are about competition, self-assurance and new industrial, urban wealth.

Our understanding of 19th-century British culture is continually hampered by an insistence on limiting the term 'Romantic' to the period 1780 to 1830, as if six poets were the whole story. This approach consigns the rest of the century's cultural achievements to the ragbag of 'Victorian literature', neglecting the art, architecture and music of the period, not mention the European context, as if the continent were cut off by

> The tendency to omit Jane Austen from considerations of Romanticism is also very telling.

about 70 years of fog. Yet it is as clear as a Constable noon that the Brontës, Tennyson, Dickens and George Eliot are Romantic novelists and poets, consciously writing within a tradition that includes Keats, Wordsworth, Austen and Scott. If we fail to understand that, we fail to understand their work. We also fail to see the connections between the apparently different Pre-Raphaelite painters and poets, and the Naturalist novelists and playwrights. We further fail to examine the usefulness of the term 'Victorian' and leave **Biedermeier** entirely out of our critical vocabulary. Yet all this comes from, contributes to or conflicts with Romanticism, as will be shown in the course of this book.

2
The idea of Romanticism

Napoleon's legacy

Napoleon is one of the major fault lines in the Romantic movement. For much of European, particularly French, Romanticism, Napoleon was an icon; in England he was a foreign menace to be feared or mocked, but rarely admired.

> It is worth mentioning at the outset one important exception to this rule: the Brontë sisters. From the date of their father's return from Leeds with wooden soldiers, Nelson, Wellington and Napoleon became part of the childhood play which in turn shaped their adult writing.

When the French poet and dramatist **Alfred de Musset** (1810–1857) wrote an elegy for the recently deceased singer Mme Malibran, he lists the painter Géricault, the composer Bellini, Goethe, Schiller, Byron, and Napoleon as geniuses whom the modern world had recently lost. What was it about Napoleon that made him not simply a politician or military tactician, but a kind of creative artist? After all, a modern British audience is likely to view him as a power-crazed dictator like Hitler who seized power through a mix of election and military coup, and went on to fight pointless wars all over Europe, ending in defeat by a combination of military alliance and Russian snow.

One key facet of his appeal was that he was a **self-made man**. He recaptured Toulon from the British in 1793, quashed a Royalist uprising in Paris in 1795 and captured Malta and Egypt in 1798. To us, this might seem too much like *Blitzkrieg* to be admired. But we forget that Napoleon's army did not see itself as an imperialist army advancing French interests, but as a revolutionary one spreading the doctrine of

> The legend that Napoleon seized the crown from Pope Pius VII to crown himself in his 1804 imperial coronation merely emphasises this aspect of his appeal. In fact, his crowning of himself and then his wife happened after the pope had blessed the regalia and according to previously-agreed procedure.

liberty, the rights of man and the downfall of tyrants. Furthermore, where the Third Reich left little behind it but a smoking pyre, the Napoleonic achievement included enduring marks on French society and European politics. The style of local government imposed on France by Napoleon did away with the Revolution's endless elected committees in favour of a prefecture system which endures to this day. It was not until the Fifth Republic that the national assemblies acquired the kind of power that they had briefly enjoyed during the First Republic (where, ironically, the British parliamentary system was seen as the model).

Perhaps as a result of Napoleon's legacy, the issue of **power** rose to the fore in French Romanticism in a way it did not in British.

That is not to say that the wider issue of **heroism** is neglected in English Romanticism. Mr Thornton in Gaskell's *North and South* is that novel's hero as much as George Knightly is in *Emma*. Rouncewell is not condemned by Dickens along with Bounderby (*Hard Times*). Nor is Sir Thomas Bertram admired for being old money: he fails to exercise sound moral judgement and entirely misreads a whole series of situations (*Mansfield Park*). What mattered was the energy and integrity of the individual, and their ability to transcend limitations of social class and respond to the demands of the situation in which they found themselves.

Generations of readers have been upset to see Mary Crawford punished, but although she has energy, like Elizabeth Bennett (*Pride and Prejudice*), she lacks integrity and shows no awareness of this lack.

The poetry of the era is characterised by a widespread regret that society's judgement of people according to their wealth was leading to, in Wordsworth's words, a '**getting and spending**' culture, or what Carlyle called the 'cash-nexus', a world in which employer owed employee nothing except

From Wordsworth's sonnet 'The world is too much with us'.

their wage at the end of the week. This was very different from the world of deference, in which the landowner was supposed to concern himself with his tenants' wellbeing. Those who could succeed in the new competition glowed with the confidence of Dickens' industrialist Mr Bounderby or politician Mr Gregsbury (*Nicholas Nickleby*), who declares his patriotism in a laborious sentence, ponderously decorated with innumerable self-satisfied sub-clauses; Britain was powerful, prosperous and full of railways, and he was proud to be a Briton. Those who got the rougher end of the deal were more likely to sound like Stephen Blackpool in the same author's *Hard Times*, who struggles to understand both his society and perhaps the plot of the novel, only to die declaring 'It's a muddle'.

Think about the implications of giving a character the name of a town that only acquired economic and political weight in the 19th century. Half a century later a dystopian novel featured a character called Tony Luton for the same reasons. Blackpool and Luton first acquired their own Members of Parliament following the 1884 Representation of the People Act.

Goethe

Born 20 years before Napoleon, **Johann Wolfgang von Goethe** (1749–1832) was perhaps the greatest voice of **Deutsche Klassik** (German Classicism). But like Beethoven, he also foresaw Romanticism and wrote an enduring definition of how the new movement differed from his generation's Classicism: if the Classical knew excess, it did not practise it; Romanticism was by contrast bound to do so.

Goethe is also the author of the seminal *Die Leiden des jungen Werthers* (*The Sorrows of Young Werther*), a book read by most of Europe's literate classes, and which shaped the perception of the Romantic artist.

Unlike Beethoven, Goethe met Napoleon and described his quality as demonic. Was Goethe trying to define him (or at least his impact) as something akin to an amoral force of nature, powerful and exciting like a volcanic eruption, to which it is useless to try to apply ethical judgements? In so doing, he set in motion a persistent Romantic theme, which one can find in Byron (to some extent) and to which Dostoevsky offers in effect a rebuttal in his Raskolnikov (*Crime and*

Punishment) and Ivan (*Brothers Karamazov*). This is a reaction against the Christian (or at least theist) assumptions in the moral philosophy of Kant; the Romantics began to realise that that if one removed that Christian element from ethical thought, anything was permitted. No one explored this idea more than Baudelaire. These are themes to which Nietzsche returned in his *Birth of Tragedy*.

> Nietzsche is available in various editions and translations. Hollingsworth (Penguin) is sound, but there is an additional interest to anything Walter Kaufman translates or comments on.

As a young man, Goethe was influenced by **folksong**, under the influence of J. G. Herder (1744–1803), and his own verses were set by Beethoven, Schubert, Schumann, Wolf and others. His novels exercised a certain influence on the development of Romantic fiction. Here is not the place to attribute labels to Goethe and Schiller (Klassik), Heine and Kleist (Romantik) as if this were a ticketing procedure. Their lives overlap to varying degrees in time, and their works do also, to

> *The Mirror and the Lamp: Romantic Theory and the Critical Tradition* by Meyer H. Abrams, Oxford University Press, 1953 (various reprints), is by a specialist in English literature, but shows awareness of the German Romantic literary debate.

varying degrees, in subject matter and tone. The agenda of passionate love, the experience of the natural world, issues of power and influence within human relationships of all kinds, responding to the arts of the ancient world: none of these things began when any one author or composer was born, nor ended when another died.

The problem, thus, is how to define Romanticism, since it was a movement which embraced all of Europe (and places which felt European influence, such as the United States of America), which ran for a century or more, and which shaped several different art forms. Each art form does not develop smoothly in step with the others; English literary studies often have subtitles that include dates like 1765–1830, which wouldn't help the music historian greatly, as 1830 is often the date cited for the beginnings of Romantic music. But although the movement was not neatly synchronised across Europe, many contemporaries knew of one another's work, and this was thus a self-conscious movement:

- Coleridge read the preceding generation of Germans and translated Schiller
- Wordsworth read the earlier Burns
- Schiller knew Goethe
- Goethe met Beethoven and Napoleon
- Poems by Goethe and Heine were set by Schumann and Schubert
- Schiller's plays were made into operas by Verdi
- Beethoven wrote an overture to one of Goethe's plays
- Géricault advised Delacroix to study Constable
- Schumann praised Brahms
- Wagner encouraged Bruckner
- Balzac read Scott
- Baudelaire read Poe
- Dostoevsky read Dickens

- Lermontov read Byron
- Clare, in his madness, occasionally thought he was Byron and even rewrote some of his poems.

There are countless other examples from every part of Christian Europe. Nevertheless, it was not a movement with an agreed manifesto like a political party:

Note that south-east Europe was under Muslim rule at this time and so has a rather different cultural history.

- Wordsworth, Baudelaire and Novalis wrote very different poetry
- Schumann and Wagner took different sides in a debate about the direction of music
- Blake was so out of step with his age that he was largely ignored for a century and only rediscovered by the age of Modernism.

Where in all this wealth is Romanticism to be found?

In this book, we shall be noting certain features that keep recurring, and pointing to these as the things by which to map Romanticism. Not every work showcases every theme or idea listed below, but these are the landmarks by which to steer:

- Childhood
- Nature
- Human experience
- The hero
- The artist
- The arts
- Beauty
- The uncanny
- Power.

As we shall show by examining a few key works, Romanticism was defined by an enquiry into what a human being actually was. They pursued this by looking at the human relationship with the natural world, and with the development of the human character and soul during childhood. As part of that enquiry, they were also concerned to look at unusual and outstanding individuals, the heroic leader, for example, who showed not what people were, but what they might become. Since as people themselves they were a part of the enquiry, artists, like the psychoanalysts of a later generation, found it important to be introspective and consider their own nature, character, development and motivation. This led to a rise in the autobiographical content of the arts.

The pose of the subject in Wallis's *Death of Chatterton*, exhibited in 1856, is surely modelled on that of Christ in a pietà. Indeed, part of the loneliness it expresses is communicated through the absence of the Virgin Mother with all that suggests about neglect and abandonment, as

Thomas Chatterton's story became known throughout Europe as an example of extraordinarily early blossoming of talent and early death. He was adept at writing in others' styles and made a living by forging Medieval poetry. Wordsworth, Coleridge, Shelley and Keats all wrote about him or dedicated poems to his memory; Alfred de Vigny wrote a play about him.

17

well as about the role of the artist in the Romantic vision. The symbols littering the painting of the dead poet, as well as the pose, the subject and the intertextual references, tell of the Romantic themes of childhood and youth, formative years, the artist, the nature of art, the status of the artist in society, the changing role of art and religion, and morbidity.

In addition, the overwhelming purpose of Wallis' painting is to demand an **emotional** reaction from the viewer. Baudelaire was the first to define Romanticism as 'une manière de sentir' ('a way of feeling') and the sense that the primary purpose of the arts was to form and draw out its reader's or audience's emotions was, though hardly new, certainly new in the centrality assigned to it.

> Cited in *Poem and Symbol: A Brief History of French Symbolism*, Wallace Fowlie, Penn State University Press 1990. Baudelaire for those without French is best read via the prose versions of Francis Scarfe which accompany a French text (Anvil).

Artists at this time were engaged in a debate, sometimes explicit, sometimes implicit in the works themselves, about the nature, purpose and role of the arts. Many tended to believe that works of art ought to be capable of encouraging people to become better, greater, more heroic – to release their hidden potential. Perhaps to that end they sought to make their works emotionally powerful, beautiful, sublime – and, in the case of music, larger, longer, brighter, louder, perhaps more heroic than anything previously written. This is one aspect in which Romanticism has continued to shape our aesthetic lives as a culture and as individuals.

A reflective movement

Perhaps unsurprisingly, this was also the great age of **artistic theory** and the beginnings of **arts journalism**. Eduard Hanslick and William Hazlitt, two of the era's most prominent music and literary critics are quoted to this day while responses to early performances and publications can be found in documents such as Pepys' diaries or Aubrey's *Brief Lives*. These did not attempt to analyse or theorise. Schumann may be seen as a conservative and Baudelaire a radical, but both men had a common interest in arts journalism. The reasons are twofold:

- Artists of previous generations were given money by wealthy aristocrats, public institutions and the Church; the collapse of the patronage system left artists casting around for sources of income
- Schumann and Baudelaire were trying to define, defend and publicise new developments in the arts.

Journalism was thus, for both men, part of their commitment to their art. Baudelaire is a notable writer on poetry and painting, Schumann was the founder editor of *Neue Zeitschrift für Musik* in which, in his last contribution, he hailed the young Brahms. His contemporary Mendelssohn was engaged in a similar campaign when he set up a music conservatory in Leipzig.

This self-reflexive concern with the artistic process itself may not be entirely new, but its centrality to artists' sense of what they were about certainly was. It is a natural extension of their concern with the questions of what a human being is and what an artist is. It goes some way to clarify what is taking place in:

- Fuseli's *The Artist Moved by the Magnitude of Antique Fragments*, where he portrays himself among the ruins of statuary
- Wallis' portrait of Chatterton
- Delacroix's and Berlioz's autobiographical writings
- Auguste Barbier's poems 'Dante' and 'Michel-ange'.

> Wallis and Fuseli are both discussed in 'Romanticism in English Art' by Marcia Pointon, in *The Romantics* ed. Stephen Prickett, London: Methuen, 1981.

The strange issue of the 'the uncanny' is another key element in the Romantic enquiry into human nature. Sometimes it can be found in the apparently rational form of historical fiction, such as the wild success of Walter Scott's novels or Flaubert's *Salammbô*. Ludwig Tieck (1773–1853), an influential German Romantic poet, is probably best known to the English-speaking world as the source of a song cycle by Brahms. *Die schöne Magelone* (The Fair Magelone) was published in 1841 as part of an anthology of poems and was based on a 16th-century German tale, itself based on an Old French Romance. Brahms' op 33 is his only song cycle and dates from the 1860s, setting 15 of Tieck's 18 poems. It contains a knight and a lady falling courteously in love, elements that we can also find in the programmes of music by Weber, for example (see page 26).

> A song cycle is a set of songs with an implicit narrative thread and characters running through them; see page 6.

Both *Jane Eyre* and *Wuthering Heights* are marked by uncanny elements. In the former there is a scene in which Jane hears a voice calling and another where she appeals to the moon goddess for help. In the latter the narrator is convinced he has seen the dead Cathy knocking on the window, and Heathcliff calls to the ghost. Sometimes uncanny elements show up in the form of ghost stories, a neglected theme within Dickens' fiction, such as 'The Signalman'. In the latter case, we should not isolate them, for they are closely linked by the style in which they are written to scenes in the apparently social and political novels. Clearly *A Christmas Carol* is a political, religious and psychological tale, not merely a ghost story. But the scenes showing the guilt felt by Ralph Nickleby (*Nicholas Nickleby*) or Bill Sykes (*Oliver Twist*) have as much of the 'uncanny' about them as the ghost fiction, even though there is nothing supernatural or occult about either plots.

> For more on the bizarre and occult, see page 31. *Dickens the Novelist*, by F. R. Leavis and Q. D. Leavis, Penguin, is both acute and conscious of Dickens' background and environment.

Medieval tales, ghost stories, nightmares, visions, and the dying insight of guilty men: what do these add up to? They are all blows struck against the humanism of the **Enlightenment**. The Enlightenment, rational child of the **Renaissance**, emphasised the human ability to solve problems through observation and the use of reason, and taught that the universe was itself ordered and reasonable. To

19

Romantics such as Tieck, this noble enterprise to understand had degenerated into the self-satisfied assumption that we now understood most things and would soon know all that remained. This, argued Tieck, was a shallow philosophy, devoid of mystery. Romanticism drew attention to the inexplicable and argued that there was much about the world and our own nature that we did not, and perhaps could not, understand. All was not light, as Alexander Pope had written in his praise of Enlightenment hero Isaac Newton. On the contrary, the external world was full of shadows — and so was our internal nature.

Indeed, John Keats (1795–1821) made a virtue of the very act of not trying to reason through a mystery or reach a conclusion to a period of doubt. 'Negative capability' is a key doctrine in his work, implying receptivity and therefore the ability to participate in life and create poetry. In two letters from 1817 he explains the importance of remaining 'in uncertainties, Mysteries, doubts, without any irritable reaching after fact and reason', and he identified Shakespeare as the great exemplar of the capability.

> Keats and Embarrassment, Christopher Ricks (OUP 1976) is short and readable.

The greatest of these shadows, or mysteries, was human passion, and the theme of falling in love came to dominate the fiction of the Romantic century to such an extent that it subsequently took over the term entirely. Today, 'romantic' literature is exclusively that of sentimental and passionate attachment. But as both Charlotte and Emily Brontë set out to show (and here at least they agree with Jane Austen), human passion is not a source of light entertainment. There is a great deal of anger, jealousy, violence and cruelty to be found in it, and the Romantic novel is often about the process of learning the essential social skills of disciplining passion, and the fatal consequences of not doing so.

The reason why Jane Austen has George Knightley praise a usefully domesticated landscape at the expense of an impressively wild one (in *Emma*) is because Austen has seen and is hostile to the beginnings of Romanticism. Her persistence in the theme of courtship is not merely because she enjoys writing about misunderstandings, quarrels and weddings, but because she is participating consciously in a debate which Romanticism had already initiated, and in her fiction an attentive reader will find many of the items on the bullet list on page 17.

> Commentators often point to Charlotte Brontë's condemnation of Austen's fiction as being too domestic and polite, but they share an agenda and even certain influences, such as Samuel Richardson.

The Romantic artist took on certain hieratic responsibilities and something of a priestly status, and there was a widespread tendency to attribute religious or spiritual value to the arts, and for the arts to adopt religious language, particularly when dealing with the natural world. For example, there is an echo of church vocabulary, the sacred idea of breath and the soul, in poetry's depictions of the wind. Wordsworth's 'Oh there is blessing in this breeze' (the opening lines of *The Prelude*, and thus the equivalent of a Homeric invocation of a muse or goddess of inspiration at the commencement of an epic), his 'The winds come to me from the fields of sleep' (*Ode, Intimations of Immortality*) and Shelley's 'O wild West

Wind, thou breath of Autumn's being' (*Ode to the West Wind*) are both about inspiration, but are both also clearly intended to recall the story of Pentecost and the theology of the Holy Spirit, invoking religious as well as artistic concepts of inspiration and expiring. Shelley goes on to remind us that the wind is a force of death ('O thou/ Who chariotest to their dark wintry bed/ The wingèd seeds, where they lie cold and low,/ Each like a corpse within its grave').

> The relationship of the sublime, or divine, and death, is of considerable significance to Romanticism, as witness the role of the funeral march to complement the heroic in music.

We shall see in the following chapters the way in which the theme of Nature is used to express beauty. It is not that the Enlightenment had no concept of beauty, nor that the 18th century lacked landscape poetry. But Romanticism develops a new theory of beauty, one which is informed by the themes of the uncanny and of power, leading to something that we call the **sublime**. With that, all the other themes are drawn together.

3
Romanticism in music

Continuity and change

Romantic composers saw themselves as trailblazers – but this is not to say they did not have enormous respect for the past. Mozart, Beethoven and, in Schumann's words, the 'insufficiently appreciated Bach' continued to exercise a significant influence. Accordingly, while some musical conventions certainly did evolve, many remained constant or changed only gradually over time.

Composers such as Berlioz, Schumann and Brahms continued to write for the Classical forms and ensembles they had inherited. The concerto, the symphony, the sonata and the opera certainly developed and became more flexible under Romanticism, but it is important to remember that all these structures were inherited from Classical composers. Indeed, throughout the Romantic era, sonata form continued to be discussed, taught, employed, developed and codified.

One important change, however, was in the range of instruments for which concertos were written, which did significantly narrow. The violin and piano thrived; other instruments fared less well, struggling to cut through the bigger, louder orchestra. Indicative of this is the fact that, from the time of Mozart to that of Strauss, almost no concertos were composed for the horn.

> Dvořák's cello concerto was an important exception, its artistic success surprising many of his contemporaries.

Winners and losers

Composers took advantage of the piano's increased responsive and expressive powers, increasingly writing solo repertoire and more imaginative Lieder accompaniments. In Schumann, Chopin and Liszt – who were also virtuoso performers – the age saw the growth of the 'pianist composer'.

> Lieder (from the German *Lied*: song) are works in which the piano partners rather than accompanies the voice.

As composers embraced nationalism in the late 19th century, operas and symphonies (or symphonic poems) emerged as the preferred mediums for conveying a sense of national identity. Examples of symphonic poems include *Prometheus* (Liszt) and *Má Vlast* (Smetana), while Mussorgsky's *Boris Godunov* is a notable example of a nationalist opera.

> A symphonic poem (or tone poem) is an orchestral work in one movement which draws upon a non-musical source, such as a poem or painting, to provide a programme.

The 19th century also saw the rise in Britain of the brass band. However, it is important to note that these tended to play arrangements of opera tunes and rarely pieces written specifically for them by composers of note.

The genres which suffered most neglect were the oratorio and the string quartet. Mendelssohn's enthusiasm for writing oratorios (*Paulus*, *Elijah*) was not one he shared with many composers of the age, although Liszt did experiment with the genre, for example in his work *Christus*.

No composer of string quartets really picked up where Haydn, Mozart and Beethoven had left off. After the death of Schubert in 1828, only Mendelssohn published a substantial contribution to the quartet repertoire. Borodin, Franck, Smetana (and later Debussy and Ravel) dipped into the medium but no composer of note succeeded in making their mark.

The Romantic orchestra
Commentators frequently draw attention to the fact that the orchestra expanded in the late 18th and 19th centuries, and this is certainly the case. Its growth should not, however, be regarded as an inevitable or organic process; it resulted from specific factors dictated by composers, instrument makers and audiences.

The increasing importance of subscription concerts as a source of income for musicians, and the corresponding growth in size of halls required to house this larger paying audience, meant the orchestra had to get bigger and its instruments louder. But this is not to say that the expansion was arbitrary, as composers

> Subscription concerts are concerts attended by a wider public and not simply by an aristocratic patron and his court.

added instruments discriminately, for their specific associations. The core of the orchestra remained the strings, as it had been since Lully, but the role of the wind went above and beyond the occasional addition of novelty and colour. The following instruments became established members of the orchestra:

- The **trombone**. This had led a relatively quiet life in the late Baroque and Classical periods but had once been part of cathedral ensembles. Its use in the orchestra might evoke solemn ceremonies in the presence of God, kings and bishops: royal funerals and great state occasions.
- The **trumpet**. As a descendant of the instruments used to announce the arrival of monarchs, and for communication on the battlefield, it invoked history, dignity and struggle.
- The **horn**. This was once a hunting instrument. As hunting was the pastime of the aristocracy, and a deliberate practice of wartime skills by a cavalry elite, it brought a sense of grandeur to the orchestra.

> The horn is French in the Anglophone world only because Britain used to import them from France.

- The **flute**. With Romanticism's increasing focus on the natural world, the flute was often used to depict the blowing of the wind.
- The double reeds, the **oboe** and **bassoon**. These had long been recognised as

> The reedy sound of the oboe and bassoon had already been exploited by Vivaldi and Mozart to paint landscapes.

possessing a rural sound. The pastoral woodwind passages in Romantic music may be drawing on memories of church music (as with the use of the trombones) as well as of folk dances.

- **Timpani.** These featured in the orchestra increasingly as the Romantic era progressed, leading the way to their prominent role in Modernist music. Perhaps the appeal of the timpani to a composer, at a time when the human struggle towards understanding and greatness was so important a cultural theme, was that its two-tone tuning to tonic and dominant allowed it to subtly invoke the two-pulse beat of the human heart. This in turn resulted in the symphony evoking more powerfully a living thing.

- The **snare drum.** This began as a military instrument. Like the sounding trumpets, it beats out a message that human life is a struggle, implying that we must expect losses, wounds and defeats, and be determined to triumph.

> These military origins are invoked by its alternative name, 'side drum', as it was worn slung to the side on the hip by regimental drummers.

It should, however, be emphasised that these wind and percussion instruments were not limited to a programmatic 'character actor' role, any more than the Romantic symphony itself was an endless recycling of the Napoleonic legend by proxy. As full members – not visitors – to the orchestra they participated fully in 'absolute music' and the process of sharing and developing musical motifs.

Beethoven's legacy

The expansion of the wind and percussion sections during the Romantic era was foreshadowed by the increasing prominence of non-string instruments in Beethoven's symphonies:

Symphony No 1: two flutes

Symphony No 3: three horns

Symphony No 5: piccolo, contrabassoon and three trombones

> It is important to recall that the Classical symphonies of Haydn and Mozart might be scored, for example, for one flute or, often enough, no flutes at all.

Symphony No 9: four horns, triangle, cymbals and bass drum.

In tandem with the increase in instrumental forces, Beethoven's symphonies grew in length – his first lasts around 27 minutes, his ninth 75 minutes. This set a standard that later composers sought to match, for the increased forces and duration did not translate simply as greater technical wealth and greater enthusiasm with which to spend it. It implied that the symphony was now a genre capable of addressing the great questions which preoccupied other art forms. The earliest examples of symphonies had emerged from German orchestral suites and Italian Baroque overtures as short, pleasant, instrumental entertainments. The Romantic symphony, however, demanded to be taken as seriously as the three-volume novel, the epic poem and the large impasto oil painting (what Constable called his 'six footers'). And, like them, it would address life.

The symphony

Commentators often say that the 19th-century agenda was drawn up by Beethoven's Symphony No 9 (perhaps because Wagner said so), but in fact the earlier part of the century was spent coping with the impact of his third, the *Eroica*.

It would be a great simplification to claim that Romantic composers wrote symphonies according to a formulaic recipe. By their very nature, great composers innovate upon and subvert tried and tested forms. However, when examining a number of Romantic and post-Romantic symphonies, a certain pattern does emerge. And you may be surprised how frequently the ingredients listed below continue to recur long after the *Eroica* helped establish this pattern.

- An intense Andante or Allegro which reflects the struggle between good and evil. The trumpet and snare drum often feature prominently.
- An Adagio, which reflects on the darker side of the struggle. This may include a formal state procession, such as a coronation or funeral, perhaps with trombones and timpani.
- A contrasting Scherzo, which evokes the brighter side of life. It may use woodwind to evoke a landscape or pastoral scene, perhaps including country dances or an impression of a river in the strings. This movement is designed to remind us that, behind the triumphs and disasters of human endeavour, there is the enduring reality of the natural world and traditional way of life.

  In Haydn's day, this is where you would expect a minuet, the sole surviving dance from the Baroque suite.
- A concluding quick movement. This draws the three movements together to end on a note of triumph. Life is depicted as a struggle, but grief and dancing both feature. In the end, heroic courage triumphs; the movement usually ends with a gallop in which the brass and percussion may echo either the chase of a hunt or a victorious cavalry charge.

Variations do occur. Sometimes the Scherzo precedes the Adagio; sometimes the mood is more cheerful in the opening movement. Brahms developed an idiosyncratic 'Intermezzo' in place of the Scherzo, a deviation which owed much to Beethoven, while Mendelssohn did not specialise in struggle (he seemed to have been, to quote Goethe, 'born under a happy constellation'). Romantic composers were not merely choosing from a short 'menu' of possible movements to construct à la carte symphonies; nor were the movements themselves creatively inert. On the contrary, there was enormous fluidity of form written in the individual categories.

Exceptions aside, this pattern's popularity and endurance shows the extent to which:

- Any creative artist is in dialogue with their times
- Power, conflict and nature were being debated in the Romantic age
- That debate was reflected in the explicit or implicit programmes of Romantic orchestral music.

Programmes in music

A debate on the comparative value of absolute and programme music raged from the time of Beethoven and throughout the Romantic period. The idea of a symphonic programme was first explicitly stated in Beethoven's *Eroica* and *Pastoral* symphonies. The former not only carried a famously destroyed dedication to Napoleon, but perhaps more importantly, quotes Beethoven's own *Creatures of Prometheus* to establish a heroic, mythological programme complete with a funeral march.

In the latter, the composer marks movements with explicit declarations of intent such as 'happy thoughts upon arriving in the countryside' and 'thanksgiving after the storm'. From here it is but a short step to Berlioz's 'Scene in the Meadows' and the other episodes in his *Symphonie fantastique*. Indeed, Berlioz invokes the rural life in ways Beethoven would have recognised: a cor anglais on stage and an off-stage oboe depict two shepherds piping to one another. Even Berlioz's famous decision to score two cornets, two ophicleides, two harps and that pastoral cor anglais for the biggest and most varied orchestra yet follows Beethoven's precedent, just as it sets a precedent for the instrumentation of Wagner, Mahler and other late Romantic composers.

> Technically a bass-keyed bugle, the ophicleide was invented in 1817 and played the role later assumed by the tuba.

A self-aware Mendelssohn himself wrote, in a satirical letter to Carl Friedrich Zelter in 1832, that a Romantic piece of music necessarily began with dreams, continued with despair, followed with a declaration of love, and ended with a march. The alternative was a dialogue between shepherd and shepherdess, a thunderstorm, a church bell and again the ubiquitous march. Weber (1786–1826) tended to keep his programmes to himself, but, in the case of his one-movement piano concerto op 79 Konzertstück, he confided it to a friend. From this, we are justified in suspecting the presence of knights and battles elsewhere in his work. **Carl Maria von Weber** (1786–1826) tended to keep his programmes to himself, but, in the case of his one-movement piano concerto op 79 Konzertstück, he confided it to a friend. From this, we are justified in suspecting the presence of knights and battles elsewhere in his work.

It is important to emphasise that music need not be 'about' something in quite the same way that novels, poems or paintings usually are. However, Western music frequently has a programme, whether implicit or explicit. During the Romantic period, as interest in linking different art forms grew, composers began to take the idea of having an underlying programme seriously.

Composers in supposedly rival sub-schools – Mendelssohn (*Midsummer Night's Dream*), Berlioz (*Roméo et Juliette*), Wagner and Liszt (*Hamlet*) – shared a profound admiration of Shakespeare and all wrote programme music that reflected his influence (or at least, their sense of what his influence ought to be). Many composers adopted literary sources: plots, characters and incidents were mined and often reflected in titles. Tchaikovsky found *Francesca da Rimini* in Dante's *Inferno* while Liszt bases one character on a late medieval Italian poet

(Tasso) and another on a medieval legend previously adapted by Goethe (Faust). The Faust story was also adopted by Gounod, Schumann and Wagner.

Hector Berlioz (1803–1869) was typical in his admiration for Shakespeare and Byron. In *Harold en Italie* he adopted a Byronic hero, while the *Symphonie fantastique* programme combines autobiographical self-expression with literary allusions (the witches' Sabbath reflects the composer's reading of *Macbeth*). The overall programme contains themes which represent characters including Napoleon (of course) and Mary Queen of Scots. Berlioz took the expression **idée fixe** from contemporary medicine to describe what is essentially a theme which recurs frequently. However, the associations of mental illness suggest something occult or psychotic, implying that it takes over and disables the composer's will.

The technique of constantly reiterating a musical theme or idea is now most closely associated with **Richard Wagner**. As operas are narratives, programmes come naturally. But Wagner took the idea of programmes further than just reflecting the underlying drama of the narrative, as any composer of operas might do. More specifically, he created themes that were clearly linked to different characters, subjects, emotions, ideas or situations. He called these themes **leitmotifs**. As with the Classical subject and serialism's note row, the leitmotif can be varied, developed, transformed and repeated; it can also be combined with another leitmotif, as dictated by the plot and the interaction of its characters.

> Nietzsche's initial enthusiasm for Wagner and later disillusionment, documented in *Das Geburt der Tragödie (The Birth of Tragedy)* and *Der Fall Wagner (The Case of Wagner)* are well worth studying as an example of a Romantic writer reflecting on Romantic music.

As Wagner's compositions were shaped by musical as well as narrative imperatives, it is not unusual to discover leitmotifs introduced to fit the needs of a particular passage of music where the narrative link to that character is hard to demonstrate. Wagner himself confessed to the influence of Beethoven, even pointing to his *Fidelio* as the piece of music that made him decide to be a composer of operas. But surely *Creatures of Prometheus*, with its mythological programme, couldn't have failed to influence Wagner's searches through Middle High German's literature for plots?

A view from abroad

Walter Scott and then Byron made Scotland unexpectedly famous, resulting in a rich musical harvest. Schumann's and Mendelssohn's *Schottische* symphonies are obvious examples. Artists looked north to the Celtic, Germanic and Norse fringes of Europe, rather than exclusively south to the warmer (Roman and Greek) Mediterranean. Those colder, wilder climes represented a part of the world which had not been under Roman imperial rule, and which offered a barer, harsher (yet still European) take on human life and human

> The novel *Frankenstein* emphasised the theme of northernness to the extent of setting scenes in the Arctic.

nature. In a Classical/Romantic polarity they seem demonstrably Romantic in nature. When *Ossian* was first published in the 18th century, he was greeted as a northern Homer. Whatever its merits or demerits as literature, it, in tandem with Scott's works, placed Scotland on the map and thus led to the composition of Mendelssohn's *Hebridean* Overture in 1830. Wagner was by no means alone in looking to Germanic mythology as a source of opera plots (see page 29).

This interest in northern-European culture reflected the Romantic fascination for the unknown. Sometimes this was expressed in a taste for the macabre, as in the Gothic novels which enjoyed a wide readership from the 18th century right through the 19th century. Sometimes it was expressed in a taste for the foreign, as demonstrated by the Spanish Gypsies in Prosper Mérimée's *Carmen* (the story on which Bizet's 1873/4 opera was based). Like literature, music sought out what critics often call 'local colour': sights and sounds that capture a sense of exoticism or foreignness. Composers continued to regard Spain as exotic, even in Ravel's time.

> We can see that Ravel was inspired by Spain from his *Alborada del gracioso* (1905/18), *L'Heure Espagnole* (1907/9) and *Rhapsodie Espagnole* (1907).

However, the Classical world was not entirely forgotten. Mendelssohn followed his *Schottische* with an *Italienische* symphony and Byron's decision to fight for Greek independence against the Turkish empire that ruled it was a direct result of his respect for Classical Greece (as well as the Romantic ideal of liberty). Perhaps most striking is Hölderlin's epistolary novel *Hyperion*, which portrays its young hero engaged in the Greek war against Turkish rule in 1770. Berlioz too went to Italy: following the example of Byron's *Harold* he wrote a work for Paganini. The soloist, however, was not impressed, and refused to play the results.

> *Hyperion* is also the hero of a lengthy poem by Keats.

Indeed, it is important to be aware of the musical Classicism inherent in the works of composers such as Mendelssohn and Brahms; the early music movement, with its performances on historically correct instruments and with the orchestral forces of the original performances, has clarified this.

> For examples of original performances, look to EMI's recordings with Richard Norrington.

This result was a conflict between Mendelssohn, Schumann and Brahms, and Liszt, Wagner and Wagnerite composers over the future of music. The latter, indeed, argued that they were writing the music of the future, claims that grated with Schumann, himself a committed champion of new music.

Yet one thing which these often diverse composers shared was an acknowledgement of the influence of literature; as we have seen, they frequently even drew upon the same sources:

- Both Schumann and Liszt wrote works based on Goethe's *Faust*

- Both Berlioz (*Harold*) and Schumann (*Manfred*) wrote works inspired by Byron.

Indeed, in 1842, Robert Schumann jotted in his notebook a startlingly prescient list of possible opera plots: Lohengrin, Nibelungen and Till Eulenspiegel. We must remember that this was some time before Wagner, let alone Strauss, composed their works on those subjects.

It was thus not so much the increased role of programmes within music that was at issue, as the other side of the compositional coin: the decreasing role of the inherited Classical forms. The adequacy of Classical forms to cater for the future needs of composers was in doubt. And it remained to be seen whether Classicism's codified rules of tonal relationships would be loosened or broken under the strain of expressing intense emotion.

The end of Classicism?

Wagner and his father-in-law Liszt did not have a monopoly on emotion. Brahms' Piano Concerto No 1 op 15 seems to obey sonata-form rules, offering the orchestra in the first exposition, the soloist in the second exposition, a development section and a recapitulation. The audience at the 1858 Leipzig premiere barely applauded: Chopin and Liszt had trained them to expect virtuoso fireworks, and the concerto was too serious for them. But this is not to say that a tragic programme did not exist. The violinist Joachim recorded that the stormy opening expressed his friend Brahms' response to the attempted suicide of Schumann. Yet the audible conflict and passion do not exclude a search for serenity. Contrast the orchestra's theme with the piano's; the development section moves from a D minor storm (grief and rage?) to a waltz (a memory of happier times?) in the tonic major, before a tragic climb to the recapitulation. Over the ensuing Adagio, Brahms wrote *Benedictus qui venit in nomine Domini*, a New Testament quotation intended as

> Latin: 'Blessed is he who comes in the name of the Lord'.

a reference to Schumann, whom Brahms had nicknamed *Mynheer Domini*, my lord and master.

Brahms had no patience with the idea that older structures were exhausted: he wrote symphonies, concertos, variations, Lieder and a range of trios, quartets, quintets and sextets. The fact that he openly alludes to Beethoven's ninth symphony in his own first (and to Schumann's third in his own third) did not mean that he did not see himself as charting new musical territory. Bruckner is generally aligned with the radical Wagner camp alongside Liszt and Hugo Wolf, in the quarrel with the supposed moderates Mendelssohn and

> Thus Brahms' first two symphonies were known to music critic Eduard Hanslick as 'Nos 10 and 11' to emphasise their links backwards to Beethoven.

Schumann. That Bruckner (b. 1824) was Brahms' (b. 1833) contemporary seems to be often forgotten, perhaps because we are so used to listening for ways in which the one looked back and the other forward, the one as Beethoven's admirer, the other as Mahler's precursor. Yet an examination of Bruckner's symphonies reveals that they look back to Beethoven's quite as much as Brahms. His adagios may well be more hymn-like than some, but then Schumann and Brahms were equally capable of drawing on the Lutheran chorale inheritance.

Looking forwards, despite Liszt's novelties, Wagner's concern with writing the 'music of the future' and the connection to that seminal modernist work, *Verklärte Nacht*, it is clear that the radicals do not have a monopoly on Romanticism's heirs. An attentive listener to Schoenberg's wonderful op 11 is more likely to spot links with Bach and Brahms than Liszt; his *Pierrot Lunaire* contains a Chopin tribute or parody. Alban Berg praised Schumann's *Kinderszenen* as an example of a piece that conceals an adventurous complexity behind a superficial simplicity.

> Schoenberg even wrote an essay called *Brahms the Progressive*, in which he also discusses his great debt to Mozart.

Liszt clearly recognised that Schumann had a 'romantic personality', attracted to the fantastic and bizarre, despite (in Liszt's terms) choosing to work with Classical forms. Similarly, while the influence on Schubert of the music of Haydn, Mozart and early Beethoven has been much commented on, his revolutionary modulations to remote keys have also attracted attention.

The Romantic question

The division into feuding camps perhaps owes more to personalities than to the works themselves. Schumann's (or more particularly, his wife's) resentment of Liszt's performing and compositional success may smack more of jealousy than judgement, but perhaps also of an uncomfortable awareness that what the radicals were doing was very close to his own work. Worse still, Liszt and Wagner tended to require admirers to be devoted disciples and followers, something Brahms, despite his interest in both men's music, was not cut out to become. Wagner, 20 years older and unable to tolerate rivals, found the applause which the younger man's work attracted agonising, and he was enraged when Brahms was awarded an honorary doctorate by the University of Breslau. Wagner also tried to solicit Mendelssohn's support and was disappointed that Mendelssohn did not advance his career. It ought to be noted that Wagner's letters sometimes refer to the need to remove the Semitic influence from German music and talk about Mendelssohn, who was Lutheran but of Jewish descent, as one of the Jews who were attacking him.

> Wagner sent Mendelssohn a copy of his early C major symphony, hoping for the latter to conduct it. He similarly solicited the admiration and support of Arthur Schopenhauer, and was disappointed yet again.

So can all these composers be defined as Romantics, or are some better described as 'Classical Romantics' or 'late Classical' composers, in the way that Mahler, Puccini, Rachmaninov, Vaughan Williams and Elgar might be called 'late Romantic', despite overlapping with the age of Modernism? To our ears, there is probably much to unite the rival composers and little to divide them. Issues of emotions in music or respect for the past don't seem divisive enough, and they all wrote programmatically. One has to accept that it was all a matter of degree. Mendelssohn, Schumann and the younger Brahms would all respond to a literary inspiration, a place or a personal experience or emotion in quite the same way as Berlioz. But they would attach greater importance to translating that into Classical musical forms and letting those forms drive the unfolding of the piece. Liszt and particularly Wagner were more willing to let traditional ideas of structure take a back seat. This is what Schumann clearly found offensive when he read through the score of *Die Meistersinger*: it all seemed a bit amateurish, the music of a man who had not been doing his harmony homework carefully enough.

> After seeing *Die Meistersinger* staged, Schumann later admitted that hearing it left a very different impression from that gained by reading it.

Romantic themes

Romanticism's concern with the **bizarre** included a flirtation with the supernatural (see, for example, Baudelaire's *Le Possédé* among many other examples). In the last movement of Berlioz's *Symphonie fantastique*, witches and monsters gather for the artist's funeral. The music combines tolling bells, bass woodwind and brass imitating the Medieval plainchant the *Dies Irae*, followed by a final witches' dance, which is wild, at least within the confines of its fugal structure. The *ff* ending to the *Symphonie fantastique* is Berlioz's equivalent of the Romantic gallop or victorious battle charge of other symphonic finales.

Mendelssohn too employed a supernatural programme, as can be seen in the Scherzo from his Octet op 20. Yet the briefest acquaintance with these two pieces is enough to show that, while each was responding to the cultural agenda of the day, each was independent in the way they interpreted this agenda. Mendelssohn's magical folk are light and airy, Berlioz's are menacing. As George Marek puts it: 'Mendelssohn represents the light, Berlioz the dark side of Romanticism'. Mendelssohn met Berlioz in Rome and judged him to be talentless, claiming he was 'groping in the dark', yet 'thought himself to be the inventor of a new world'. He was, he wrote to his mother, a 'poseur'. Berlioz took to Mendelssohn (almost everyone did), merely being entertained that the German should take his Lutheran faith seriously.

> Further comparisons can be made between Mendelssohn's *Midsummer Night's Dream* and Berlioz's *Queen Mab*.

There is no need to labour the point about the importance of **nature** in Romantic music. From Schumann's *Waldszenen* op 82, through the *Rheinisch* symphony, to the sea music in Wagner's *Tristan* and *Fliegende Holländer*, we observe the same sense that Charlotte Brontë expressed in her condemnation of Austen, that the arts must take the reader outdoors, away from the study, the library and the imprisonment of human society.

> Baudelaire makes a specific link between music and the sea: *La Musique souvent me prend comme une mer!* ('La Musique').

The emphasis on landscapes led composers, perhaps inevitably, to think and write about their homelands. Schumann's pianistic woodland thus becomes Smetana's *Bohemia's Woods and Fields*; his orchestral river becomes MacCunn's *Land of the Mountain and the Flood*, as Romanticism embraces nationalism (of which more later). And although it is easy to fall into the trap of linking

> Woodland seems to have a particular significance in German culture, partly due to the reminder of the ancient forest that once covered so much of the country. It implies an imagined Germany at one level, and real human nature at another.

music to programmes a little too insistently, the delicate counterpointing of the soloist by the winds in the Adagio of Brahms' violin concerto (listen for that telltale oboe, the horns and flutes) is surely an example of the individual being embraced, supported and comforted by their environment.

It is easy and uncontroversial to define the pastoral elements in 19th-century music as essentially Romantic. The heroic and epic elements, in the shape of the military and hunting themes and instruments employed, can similarly be described in terms of the orchestra's expansion. The theme of **childhood**, however, is more difficult to pin down.

> The early Romantic cult of prodigies predates Romanticism in the form of Mozart, but is still worth remarking upon. Rimbaud completed his literary work by the end of his teens, following which he abandoned both literature and Europe. Chatterton's posthumous fame was due in part to his fitting the image of a prodigy.

Early examples of writing for and about children are Schumann's *Kinderszenen* (Scenes of Childhood, 1838) and *Album für die Jugend* (Album for the Young, 1848). His three sonatas (op 118) were written for his daughters and have titles such as *Gypsy Dance* and *Doll's Cradle Song*. A late-Romantic example is Debussy (1862–1918), who makes the transition from Romanticism to Modernism with disconcerting ease. For our purposes we should simply draw attention to his *Children's Corner* piano suite (1906/8) as reflecting the Romantic concern with childhood. Another example is Humperdinck's *Hansel und Gretel* (1893), which was written both for children and about children, as was Tchaikovsky's *Nutcracker* (1891–1892), which has become as much a landmark of the musical year as Handel's *Messiah*.

New demands, new ensembles

Romantic composers wrote for children in the same way that Baroque and early Classical composers wrote for the talented amateurs who were their patrons. As the patronage system unravelled, the middle classes and their children who took instrumental lessons set the agenda for works not intended for the concert hall.

The loss of the talented amateur patron also changed the nature of music written for small ensembles. The difficulty and frequency of virtuosic passages increased, as there was no need to allow for one of the players to be clumsier (but richer) than the others. This trend towards increasing technical difficulty was supported in the case of the string quartet by technical developments which rendered the viola and cello more playable. This is a long story, but among other changes, the strings were not so thick and clumsy as they had been in the Baroque period, and accordingly players could play more quickly, more accurately and more expressively.

Secondly, the range of music written for small ensemble changed, especially with the arrival of the piano in a huge number of wealthy middle-class homes. This created a vast market for piano repertoire and music for small ensembles that included a piano. **Biedermeier** was the derogatory name given to a mid-19th-century German style that insisted on domesticity and respectability, and tended towards self-satisfaction. It's not a term one enjoys linking to genius, but it may be worth looking out for a whiff of cosy safety in the music of Mendelssohn and Schumann, especially in music written for private performance at home. Biedermeier is a culture that teaches privatising morality, avoidance of the public sphere, contentment with one's lot in life, and pleasantly (perhaps a little fussily) decorating one's home. There is much to recognise here for the British student of Victorian style and values.

> Nevertheless, in his contributions to the *Neue Zeitschrift für Musik*, Schumann was as keen in his attack of the mediocrity of Biedermeier salon composers as Baudelaire was on the poverty of poetic invention.

In music, Biedermeier culture was partly responsible for the success of **Lieder**. Of course, both Haydn and Beethoven had written Lieder, but the idea that a composer could be famous for his songs would have been as alien to an 18th-century composer as the idea of becoming famous for solo piano music. Yet Schubert, Schumann and Wolf were all examples of the former, and Schumann, Chopin and Liszt of the latter. Lieder are highly personal statements, involving a single voice, speaking as a single individual, expressing that individual's views and experiences. The loneliness of some of these characters is thus an integral feature of the genre and part of the Romantic concept of life. The union of music and poetry is also a direct expression of the Romantic commitment to articulating literary concepts in music.

Similarly, the piano sonata contrasts with the symphony or opera by showcasing one lone voice. Looking back on Beethoven's work across the Romantic period, it is hard not to see Beethoven's cycle of piano sonatas as a collection of letters or a kind of musical journal, the equivalent of Van Gogh's series of self-portraits at the close of the century. This view is certainly coloured by later developments in the arts, but it is true that, with Beethoven, the use of the piano exceeded anything the Classical period had produced. Chopin, Liszt and Schumann were all as indebted to Beethoven's piano legacy as Brahms, Bruckner and Schumann were to his symphonic one. Schumann was aware of this potential in piano music, confiding to Friedrich Wieck that when he played music by Schubert he felt as if he were reading a diary. In the case of Chopin, Schumann heard the 'deep mourning' of Polish nationalism: it contained a public, implicitly political, statement but was intensely personal for Chopin who was seen as an exile, and thus a Romantic outsider. In writing for the piano, Chopin had found the perfect medium.

The theme of the individual struggle and the heroic voice are also to be found, perhaps most dramatically, in the Romantic concerto. Brahms', Tchaikovsky's and Sibelius' violin concertos, and Dvořák's cello concerto implicitly cast the orchestra as the world and the soloist as the individual in a way that would have mystified composers of the Baroque era. Sometimes the orchestra supports the soloist as a Friedrich landscape would smile on the passing walker: in the Dvořák, such was the interplay of instruments that a *Musical Times* critic called the piece 'three orchestral movements with violoncello obbligato'. Sometimes the soloist finds a friend, as an individual instrument partners it for a while (for example, the oboe in the Dvořák). At other times the soloist struggles with an orchestra which is temporarily a hostile force, a storm more reminiscent of Géricault than Friedrich. In Brahms' violin concerto, the opening Allegro shows struggle in its double stopping and in the threatening undercurrents in the orchestral texture ; note also the military effects, some of which return in the concluding Allegro.

For a discussion of Géricault's and Friedrich's portrayals of nature, see page 49.

4
Romanticism in Literature

In Britain, it is fair to say that Wordsworth and Coleridge set the agenda for 19th-century literature with their joint publication of *Lyrical Ballads* in 1798 – considered by many to mark the starting point of English Romantic literature. The subject of **childhood**, as defined in Wordsworth's short poem, *My Heart Leaps Up*, was of particular significance because it was:

- A time of the expression of **natural identity**, before the self had been artificially shaped by social forces
- A time of **natural piety**: the child was uninhibited in its response to the natural world, and by extension to the divine creator of that world, as in:

> *Our birth is but a sleep and a forgetting*
> *Not in entire forgetfulness*
> *And not in utter nakedness,*
> *But trailing clouds of glory do we come*
> *From God, who is our home.*

Ode: Intimations of Immortality.

Hölderlin's short poem beginning *Da ich ein Knabe war (When I was a lad)* similarly links childhood with an awareness of nature and of the divine.

- A focus for thoughts on the role of **memory** in the formation of **identity**
- Of **political significance**: children own shares in a political future, as they do in a spiritual past.

The theme of childhood and growing up is a key item on the Romantic agenda and closely related to that of **nature**. Coleridge records taking pleasure in the free play of his children, Derwent and Hartley, as they ran shouting through wind-tossed trees. In his poem *Frost at Midnight*, Coleridge shows himself as an adult, promising his sleeping baby child :

> *For I was reared*
> *In the great city, pent 'mid cloisters dim,*
> *And saw nought lovely but the stars and sky*
> *But thou, my babe! shalt wander like a breeze*
> *By lakes and sandy shores, beneath the crags*
> *Of ancient mountain, and beneath the clouds.*

As academic Jonathan Cook shrewdly points out, Coleridge's contemporary, the philosopher James Mill, would have been shocked at this wasted opportunity: the boys should have been indoors being taught something useful.

Despite Mill's and Coleridge's ideological differences, they were true contemporaries in their understanding of the key importance of the formative years. Another contemporary on this count, although one little read in his own time, was William Blake. Childhood forms a central philosophical, theological and political theme in his *Songs of Innocence and Experience*.

From personal to political

The leap from the subject of childhood in English writing and painting to France's imaginative responses to Napoleon (and other historical leaders such as Caesar and Anthony) may seem implausibly large. However, if we look at both

> In David's painting of Napoleon crossing the alps, the names Bonaparte, Hannibal and Carlus Magnus (Charlemagne) are cut into the rocks.

these concerns carefully they clearly follow the same line of enquiry, namely 'What is a human being?'. The role of the child in the family invites parallels with that of the citizen in the state: an investigation into the nature of the family is thus an enquiry into the workings of the state. Blake is explicit about this double function, as the briefest glance at his chimney-sweeper poems will reveal. Turn from those to *Holy Thursday* and you find Blake exploring the social question further, investigating the psychology and theology behind acts of Christian charity. Dickens similarly explored social issues; his political stance is set out most famously in *Bleak House*.

The debate on personal and political liberty conducted in Britain following the American and French revolutions was sometimes expressed in terms of what were then called 'liberties'; a leftover in the British constitution.

> Liberties is a constitutional term relating to a town's political status.

Symbols of advance such as these could sometimes turn into symbols of restraint: the word 'chartered' in Blake's *London* would also repay study, as it clearly echoes the contemporary debate over the value or otherwise of a town acquiring its own political representative. Blake's poems reveal that he saw religious, political and psychological issues as all being on the same agenda. This may seem to us a strikingly modern understanding of all three (is this why he was marginalised in his own time?), but it was prefigured, as was so much Romantic ideology, by Rousseau. In his novel *Emile*, Rosseau insisted that:

> For further discussion of Blake's political stance, see 'Blake: Active Evil and Passive Good' by David Punter, in *Romanticism and Ideology: English Writing 1765–1830*, ed. David Aers, Jonathan Cook, David Punter, Routledge and Kegan Paul 1981.

> *Those who desire to treat politics and morals apart from one another will never understand either.*

The Bildungsroman

Bildungsroman is a German term meaning 'education novel', one which traces the development of a central protagonist from childhood to adult life. The expression was adopted in England after Goethe's *Wilhelm Meister* became known and was imitated by Thomas Carlyle (its translator) in his work *Sartor Resartus*. Childhood is of massive importance in English fiction after Wordsworth. *Jane Eyre*, *Silas Marner*, *David Copperfield* and

> See Cook's 'Romantic Literature and Childhood', in *Romanticism and Ideology: English Writing 1765–1830*, ed. David Aers, Jonathan Cook, David Punter, Routledge and Kegan Paul 1981.

countless other novels follow the Bildungsroman format, telling the story of a young girl or boy, their early experiences and how those shaped them as an adult. *Silas Marner* makes the link with Wordsworth explicit, as he is quoted on the title page as the book's epigraph.

The opening pages of Dickens' *Hard Times* – which, typical of the Romantic novel, begins in a schoolroom – offer his attack on the restrictive approach to childhood recalled in J. S. Mill's autobiography. Dickens' concern is with the true nature of humanity, its true destiny. He is diagnosing the poison of an educational system, an economic system and a social system that kills our humanity and perverts our nature. Bitzer's cold betrayal of his schoolmaster, Bounderby's pomposity, Blackpool's being sent to Coventry and Gradgrind's failure to recognise his children's true needs are all symptoms of a country where society, education and the economy have gone awry.

This is not to say, however, that the Bildungsroman was an overly formulaic genre which failed to evolve and undergo modification. Dickens is a virtuoso at challenging our sense of who a novel's hero really is, by tracing the development of Gradgrind and the older Dombey, where Romantic convention suggests the heroes ought to be their children Tom and Paul (the anonymous son of the title). Although one novel opens with Paul's birth and the other in Tom's classroom, to the extent that both are Bildungsromanen, it is the fathers who grow and change.

See *Dombey and Son*, 1846.

The dual focus on the child and its parents, and on the worker and his employer, is something which Dickens shared with George Eliot in *Silas Marner*. This novel tells the twinned stories of Silas, cast out from his own chapel and seeking a new family, and the foundling Eppie whom he adopts. In this short novel, a child is given almost messianic status, as she is able to reconcile Silas, after a long period of self-imposed reclusion, with his life, with the Church and thus with both human society and his own religious sense. Eppie counsels Silas as Louisa rebukes Gradgrind: the fact that children can hold adults to account or offer spiritual guidance is a clear mark of Romanticism's revolutionary content. *Silas Marner* also strays from Bildungsroman convention by replacing the traditional first person narrator with a more impersonal, omniscient one.

As stated earlier, closely linked with the theme of childhood is that of **nature**. Wordsworth wrote of how the natural world was a resource for the modern soul, restoring it when it had been disordered by the stresses and strains of urban life. Wordsworth's reflection on how 'getting and spending we lay waste our powers' (from his sonnet '*The world is too much with us*') is one to which our age of ambition can easily respond. His contrast between how we feel in the hurly burly of London and how we feel in the refuge of the Lake District is not only of enduring relevance to the modern world, it is also of structural importance to 19th-century literature. Indeed, the concluding lines of *The Prelude* suggest that it was Wordsworth's meditation on nature and the sublime that led him away from his early political views and enthusiasm for the French Revolution).

When he writes about daffodils, Wordsworth is thus doing more than merely saying that they look pretty. The whole point is that the memory of the daffodils (cited in the final stanza) stays with the poet and becomes part of him. Nature here is thus not merely the environment through which we pass, but a force which shapes us as clearly as we shape it.

> Nature as a refuge continues to be a living theme right through into the work of Yeats, whose famous *The Lake Isle of Innisfree* poem is built on this dialectic.

Memory

Memory was a key concern of the Romantic movement. Of course, there had been novels exploiting memory before: *Robinson Crusoe* is the most famous of a series of 18th-century novels that adopt the appearance of memoirs. What was new after Wordsworth and Coleridge, however, was that the process of remembering is in itself significant. The post-Wordsworthian novel seeks both to dramatise and to analyse the forces that shape our identity. What we were as a baby, a child or a youth is different from what we are as an adult: how does all that experience add up to some kind of identity: who and what are we?

This 'ontological insecurity', as critics call it, strikes a new note in English fiction and, however different Brontë, Eliot and Dickens may be, they are alike in finding in the Wordsworthian theme of remembering the answer to the mystery. The person who we are is the sum of our memories, and the point of writing an autobiography is not (as it was for past ages) to set down a record of our achievements for posterity to admire, nor to list the deeds of the famous with whom we have mingled, nor to show the grace of God active in our lives as it had been for the 17th-century Puritan autobiographers. It was rather a dramatic voyage of discovery, a journey in search of the self.

> John Bunyan's *Grace Abounding to the Chief of Sinners* is the most famous example of the Puritan genre, but there are many more.

A journey of the self

This is a point at which English- and French-language Romanticism converge, for the theme of voyage is of some significance in Baudelaire and others writing in the mid-19th century. Dickens does not send *David Copperfield* to the high seas, but he does indicate the theme of search in the opening sentence:

> *Whether I shall turn out to be the hero of my own life, or whether that station will be held by anybody else, these pages must show.*

As in *Hard Times* and *Dombey and Son*, Dickens is playing with the Romantic novel's conventions of introducing the hero. Similarly, Flaubert's *Madame Bovary* opens in a schoolroom, but Romantic convention is subverted in two important ways. Firstly, the original narrator, a classmate who tells the story of Charles Bovary's early school years, is quickly and ambiguously replaced by an omniscient, impersonal narrator. Secondly, Flaubert anticipates the greater ontological uncertainty of the Modernist age by having the initial narrator claim of the protagonist 'None of us remember a thing about him'.

The idea of journey fed into the French Romantics' focus on the sea and the river, to the extent that they are almost the main characters in Rimbaud's *Le Bateau ivre*, and are of primary significance in several of Baudelaire's poems, most notably *'Le Voyage'*, 'Un Voyage à Cythère' and 'L'Invitation au Voyage'. This was of course an age of travel and trade, in which oceans were crossed and fortunes made – Rimbaud himself went from writing about a journey to going on an ill-fated voyage to Africa. The existence of other places and other historical moments haunts the French imagination at this time: 'what is so special about us and what is so right about our attitudes?' is the implicit question, a concern inherited from that progenitor of Romanticism, Rousseau. In other words, it was not enough to scrutinise and catalogue current fashion and practice, it was essential to see through them to the real nature of humanity that they partly reveal and partly conceal. This was the concern, to find a human reality independent of time and place, that united such unlikely fellow Romantics as Baudelaire and Manet, Brontë and Rimbaud.

Wordsworth, encouraged by Coleridge to think of himself as a philosophical poet (which of course he was), set out to write a philosophical poem. *The Recluse* was to be a major statement, a vast poem to stand beside both the long poems of previous ages – *Paradise Lost*, *The Fairy Queen*, *The Canterbury Tales* – and the literature and symphonies of its own time. In preparation (both for himself and for the reader), Wordsworth decided to declare his own hand and put himself personally on the line by writing an autobiographical poem. As things turned out, volume 2 of *The Recluse* was written but Wordsworth never completed volumes 1 and 3. However, Wordsworth's autobiographical poem (published as *The Prelude* after his death) turned out to be a major philosophical work in its own right, for here Wordsworth pulled together all his themes into a single narrative.

> *The Prelude* is the subject of considerable scholarly debate as it underwent endless redrafting in the course of Wordsworth's life. Penguin published a dual edition of the 1805 and 1850 'editions' but it is important to remember that neither of these is actually definitive.

The aesthetics of revolt

Despite his awareness (in part through the voracious reading and conversation of Coleridge) of European, particularly German literature and thought, and despite his own travels in France at the time of the Revolution, it was not Wordsworth whose name echoed around Europe. When Byron, in his own words, woke to find himself famous, it was quickly a European fame. Like Poe's importance to French poetry, relative to his more modest standing at home in America, so Byron's standing in Germany and Russia has consistently baffled his fellow countrymen.

> Thus Mario Praz, who has much to say about Byron in his enduring study *La carne, la morte e il diavola nella letteratura romantica*, 1930 (translated as *The Romantic Agony* 1933), never mentions Wordsworth.

This inconsistency is, however, explained when we realise that his subject matter chimed more strongly with the mainland agenda than it did with the domestic one. His embattled heroes, Manfred, Harold, Juan, had their admirers in Britain of course: Esther Lyon in Eliot's *Felix Holt* was a (fictional) example. But Eliot's own views are probably better expressed in the eponymous hero's contemptuous observations: 'A misanthropic debauchee… whose notion of a hero was that he should disorder his stomach and despise mankind.' Nevertheless, one might consider whether Holt is not himself something of a Byronic hero.

> *Felix Holt*, chapter 5. Note that Eliot refers to Wordsworth in the opening of this novel. Holt's dismissal is curiously close to Rimbaud's assessment of what a poet needed to do in preparation for great work: see page 58.

Byron's subject is the revolted man, the individual who is in open conflict with his own society and times, and this put him in alliance with figures as different as the young Goethe, Pushkin and Lermontov, Baudelaire and Rimbaud. Lermontov's view of himself as a wanderer and outsider was shaped by his reading of Byron's poetic fictions, and for Pushkin the role of the outsider became a political reality when he became the object of police surveillance.

> Tsar Nicholas I appointed himself Pushkin's censor.

It would be a mistake, however, to think that Romantic writers were opposing all previous literature and attempting a complete break with the past. All the writers listed in the previous paragraph put Shakespeare on a pedestal. Wordsworth had the highest opinion of Spencer and Milton; when Coleridge wrote in praise of Wordsworth's *Prelude*, he did so in terms that subtly echo Marvell's poem on Milton's *Paradise Lost*. Romanticism's relationship with the previous age of Classicism was, however, more ambiguous. In Britain, Byron adored Pope and some authorities have argued that Pope's influence can be found in Wordsworth.

Many authorities have found the roots of English Romanticism in 18th-century authors such as Edward Young (*Night Thoughts*), James Thompson (*The Seasons*), Thomas Gray (*The Deserted Village*) and Dyer (*Grongar Hill*), with their landscapes and philosophical musings. In German literature, however, the advent of the new movement was less a gentle transition and more an artistic upheaval. This is partly due to that fact that the previous generation's marked Neoclassicism, most notably in the writings of Lessing, Schiller and the post-*Werther* Goethe, seemed more antithetical to the expression of emotional extremes which so characterised the Romantic movement. And so Tieck, Novalis and countless other writers, declaring Neoclassical forms and Enlightenment rationality stultifying, inauthentic and ignorant of life's mysteries, sought a more dramatic break with the past than their English counterparts had. And this, in turn, goes some way to explain why Germany felt a greater affinity with Byron's revolted heroes than his homeland.

Nature in literature

Look through any anthology of 19th-century French poetry, and you will quickly

begin to notice certain words which recur time and again: *montagnes*
(mountains), *lacs* (lakes), *fleuves* (rivers), *cieux*
(skies), *nuages* (clouds), *vents* (winds), *astres*
(stars), *rêves* (dreams), *soupirs* (sighs), *forêts*

For more on fogs and clouds, see page 52.

(forests), *arbres* (trees), *bois* (woods), and often enough *saules* (willows) and
bruyères (moors). This list of natural features indicates that poets pictured
themselves going for walks in the uncultivated countryside, like the hiker in
Friedrich's *Der Wanderer über dem Nebelmeer* (*The Wanderer above the Sea of
Clouds*). The *saules* and *bruyères* in particular remind us that this is economically
useless territory. In Jane Austen's *Emma* (1816), the hero George Knightley takes
issue with the pretentiousness of his neighbour's suggestions for a picnic.
Compare the neighbour's more typically Romantic view of the outdoors with
Knightley's mannered response, which is more redolent of a Classical world
view:

> *There is to be no form or parade – a sort of gipsy party – we are to
> walk about your gardens, and gather the strawberries ourselves, and
> sit under trees; and whatever else you may like to provide, it is to be all
> out of doors – a table spread in the shade, you know. Everything as
> natural and simple as possible. Is not that your idea?*

> *Not quite. My idea of the simple and natural will be to have the table
> spread in the dining-room, the nature and simplicity of gentlemen and
> ladies with their servants and furniture, I think is best observed by
> meals within doors.*

Feminist critic Marion Butler, in her epoch-making *Jane Austen and the War of
Ideas* (1975) was one of the first to explore the way in which Austen engaged in
the political and philosophical debates of her time, despite the long tradition of
regarding her novels as safe places where
nothing ideological would spoil the reader's
flight from the reality of life. Commenting on
her work, Marxist critic Terry Eagleton summed it
up as proving that Austen was a self-avowed

Commenting on Eagleton's review, Butler was rather cool about his assessment of her argument, but did not dismiss it entirely.

conservative. This may be an unnecessary generalisation, but we can be quite
clear in this case that a character Austen approves of is finding fault with the cult
of wildness, of which Wordsworth and Coleridge were card-carrying members.

This, however, is not entirely surprising: Austen and other British conservatives
associated the new forces of Romanticism with
the French Revolution and its slaughter. Critics
have traditionally been reluctant to examine
Austen's social message, perhaps because while
the quality of writing was admired, conservatism
was out of fashion in academic circles. Butler's
intention was to show that Austen's books
contained frequent indications of social and

Romanticism and Ideology: English Writing 1765–1830, ed. David Aers, Jonathan Cook, Jonathan Punter, Routledge and Kegan Paul 1981. Note the dates in the subtitle: the question of when Romanticism was effective and where is one to keep an eye on.

political opinions, and that her work is better understood if studied in the context

41

of the political currents of the time and compared to other late 18th- and early 19th- century writers: 'she was, in fact, a partisan'. As a result, Butler is concerned to show not only how Austen is in dialogue with Jacobin and anti-Jacobin writers of the time (those who espoused and those who attacked the politics of the French Revolution), but also how she is teaching a social lesson. But David Aers, another critic who follows up Butler's approach, takes up the issue of Emma's patronage of Harriet Smith. He points to the paragraph where Emma decides to advance Harriet, and the snobbery of her attitude to the Martins. Given that the Martins are substantial tenants of Domwell, they are clearly colleagues of the land-owning class, and natural allies of Emma. She is not only morally wrong in her decision to shun them, she is also socially (economically and politically) wrong, which is Aers' point.

A changing society

The issue of social class and the alliances which formed between social classes is a frequently recurring one in Romantic fiction. Little wonder: at the end of the 18th century one French class had been beheaded by another, and there were frequent variations on this head-chopping theme at different times and in different places throughout the Romantic century. In France, a social class that ought to have had a vested interest in slowing the pace of change (the bourgeoisie) had been excluded from the decision-making process, and had therefore thrown in its lot with the disenfranchised. Edmund Burke, whose analysis of the French Revolution prefigures the work of sociologists and historians a century and a half later in its detail and shrewdness, was quite clear that the revolution stemmed from the failure of the ruling class to embrace talent from outside its own ranks. Thus Romantic fiction includes, time and again, at least one outsider. A prime example of this is Fanny Price in *Mansfield Park*, the poor relation of the wealthy Bertrams who grows up in slipshod surroundings but learns the social refinements of her cousins (while at the same time being forced to remain modest and demure).

A tale of two heroines

We should compare Fanny Price's lot to that of Jane Eyre, another victim of charity and pity. Unlike Fanny, Jane cannot accept her state and spends her life in search of independence. Even in the famous declaration 'Reader, I married him' we are struck by the active verb: marriage is active not passive; she is not subservient; she is emotionally, socially (and implicitly sexually) an active partner who has made an active choice.

In this she is very close to her sister's heroine Catherine Earnshaw in *Wuthering Heights* whose declaration to Nelly 'I am Heathcliff! I cannot life without my life! I cannot live without my soul' implies a level of emotional and sexual desire quite beyond anything that our understanding of the lives of 19th-century women conventionally allows for.

The huge difference between *Jane Eyre* and *Wuthering Heights* is that Jane succeeds in domesticating Rochester's (and her own) wildness, while Catherine's and Heathcliff's wildness remains untamed and thus destructive. Only in the second generation can their love succeed; it is as though only a variation on the musical theme can reach the novel's equivalent of a perfect cadence: marriage. The end of the novel, however, is in the hands of the sexless, emotionally incompetent Lockwood. His concluding declaration that he 'wondered how anyone could ever imagine unquiet slumbers, for the sleepers in that quiet earth' is a false note if ever there was one. We have learnt painfully that Catherine and Heathcliff could never be at peace; it would be like trying to turn the heath into a kitchen garden.

> This marriage is also symbolic, reconciling the conflicting worlds and social codes implicit in the Heights and the Grange.

Socially, Heathcliff (another outsider) seeks to seize control over the house and land, and succeeds in his ambition, becoming a landowner. The same ambition to break into society and acquire money, status and land fires Balzacian heroes. Eugene de Rastignac, however different from Heathcliff, is built on the Napoleonic model: life is a war; courage, resourcefulness and ruthless ambition triumph. Furthermore, he has luck: he wins at gambling. Bounderby is also pretending to be such a character, but he turns out in fact to be twinned with La Baronne Delphine de Nucingen and her sister La Comtesse Anastasie de Restaud (*Le Père Goriot*). Stendal's Julien Sorel (*Le Rouge et le Noir*) is another young man of talent in search of advancement. The two-tone title is a reminder that the red-uniformed Napoleonic army (le rouge) no longer offers advancement and, in a society that has lost its dynamism, only the black-clad Church (le noir) offers a classless route to the top, a route for which his own nature is unfortunately ill-suited.

> De Rastignac originally appears in *Le Père Goriot*, but appears in various other works of Balzac's *Comédie Humaine*.

In *Great Expectations*, the question of social success, and the confusions which surround this, is explored in the life of Philip Pirrip (Pip). He believes himself to be the adopted son of Miss Haversham, a member of the landowning class, and that he is thus being advanced into that class by one of its own. In fact, he discovers that the ex-convict Magwitch is funding his education, living out his own fantasies of social success through Pip. Dickens, whose message is consistently the interdependence of social classes, could not have chosen a more challenging variation on the entryist theme.

> The hint of the occult in the convict-benefactor's name is a typical Dickensian touch, as is the Gothic initial encounter in a graveyard.

Society and morality

Unlike Pip, *Mansfield Park*'s Fanny Price is adopted and advanced by a bona fide member of the landowning class. Her final reward, and her cousins' contrasting punishment, are determined according to the Puritan model. Like the heroine of Richardson's *Pamela* (1740/1), which Austen had read, Fanny remains loyal to her moral code, refusing to marry for economic advantage despite the warning of her mother's example, and also refusing to marry a man not in control of his own emotions.

This lack of control (which her cousins demonstrate) is seen as more than a social weakness, it is a moral evil. The presence of evil was of course nothing new in literature, however it was Richardson who domesticated evil in the novel into something more like human wickedness. Richardson's *Clarissa* (1748/9) adapted Milton's portrait of Satan in *Paradise Lost* and successfully cast him as a pleasant, well-mannered but unprincipled aristocrat (Lovelace) who flirts with a young woman (Clarissa) and becomes so obsessed by her beauty and virtue that he ends up kidnapping and raping her. In Richardson's earlier *Pamela*, Lovelace's predecessor, Mr B. (never named in full), eventually abandons seduction and proposes marriage to his late mother's virtuous maid. This is more than a Cinderella story, it is a Christian parable assuring the poorer classes that they can achieve success in this world *and* the next by having a clear moral code and living by it. In the later wild romps of Gothic fiction, the wickedness of Lovelace was explored for its own sake, not for its contrast with Clarissa's virtue. Baudelaire's analysis of the human situation undermined the facile clarity of the distinction between good and evil, substituting instead a contrast between what is true and false.

> Richardson's contemporary Fielding belonged to the very class into which these Richardsonian heroines marry, and he detested what he saw as calculated upward mobility. His life as a novelist began in savaging Richardson, first in *Shamela* and then in *Joseph Andrews*.

> Tellingly, Loveless was also the name of a Cavalier poet of the 17th century, and thus associated with an aristocracy in conflict with more middle class values in the Civil War

Romantic novelists picked up the disturbing twin themes of human evil and evil's humanity, in characters as different as Brontë's Heathcliff (*Wuthering Heights*) and Dostoevsky's Raskolnikov (*Crime and Punishment*). Both are selfish and violent, despite their intermittent charm and obvious intelligence. Recalling the theme of exoticism and wildness, we should note that Heathcliff is dark-skinned and found in Liverpool, the home of the slave trade. Similarly, *Jane Eyre*'s Mrs Rochester (Rochester's secret wife, confined in the attic) comes from the West Indies. Whether or not we are intended to think of either of these characters as mixed race, we are surely intended to see a link with an unknown, and then unknowable, African world, a world in which the Romantics believed that the uncivilised nature of humanity could be seen.

A novelistic tradition was already available to Charlotte and Emily Brontë when it came to constructing morally dubious male characters. Richardson's Lovelace (tellingly pronounced 'loveless') is one of Mr Rochester's literary ancestors, men who are rich, who expect to get their own way, and who do not take other people's lives and feelings seriously. However, where *Clarissa* showed Lovelace unredeemed, a victim of his own greed, appetites and passions, Charlotte Brontë takes the opposite course and saves Rochester, but she does not do so by sacrificing Jane Eyre's independence. This is what the American poet and feminist

Adrienne Rich finds so exciting in the novel. Virginia Woolf dismissed Jane as 'always a governess and always in love' and compared the book unfavourably with *Wuthering Heights* because of the latter's insistence on the

The Common Reader, Virginia Woolf, 1925.

third person: 'When Charlotte wrote she said with eloquence and splendour and passion "I love", "I hate", "I suffer"... But there is no "I" in *Wuthering Heights.*'

But Rich points to the feminist politics in Jane's declarations. She quotes Jane: 'I have as much soul as you — and full as much heart!' and refers to her insistence that on standing at the feet of God, she was Rochester's equal. Rich comments angrily 'Always a governess and always in love? Had Virginia

'Jane Eyre: The Temptations of Motherless Woman', in *On Lies, Secrets and Silence: Selected Prose,* Adrienne Rich, *1966–1978,* 1980.

Woolf really read this novel?' The book's implicit feminist agenda not surprisingly is to Rich's taste; its Victorian language had somehow concealed it from Woolf.

In *Jane Eyre* we can see an insistence on self-determination that reaches back to the same politics as the French Revolution, which sparked not only Paine's *Rights of Man* (1791) but also Mary Wollstonecraft's *A Vindication of the Rights of Woman* (1792).

A fictional autobiography and Bildungsroman, *Jane Eyre* also challenges the assumptions of Christian society, not least by invoking a vision of a female divinity when Jane is advised by the moon, a clear symbol of the mother goddess. *Jane Eyre* is thus about power and nature, reflecting the Brontës' reading of Byron and Wordsworth, and their childhood play with figurines of Napoleon and Wellington.

The aesthetics of revolution

Just as the young Wordsworth praised Toussaint, so his friend, the young Coleridge, wrote in celebration of the storming of the Bastille ('The Destruction of the Bastille'), that iconic moment in the French Revolution. The terms in which he does so are very telling: he manages to praise the achievements of personifications of Freedom and Liberty without specifying actions of any kind, in part by depending on intransitive verbs. This absence of objects means that the achievement is a victimless one. Contrast this with the way in which Shelley responds to the 1819 'Peterloo' killings:

> I met murder along the way—
> He had a mask like Castlereagh
> Very smooth he looked, yet grim—
> Seven blood-hounds followed him. . .
> He tossed them human hearts to chew
> Which from his wide cloak he drew

'The Mask of Anarchy', 1789.

Coleridge's politics are visionary and seemingly detached from the world of cause and effect where people lose their heads. Similarly, Wordsworth uses intransitive verbs when striving to express the sublime in his poetic response:

> ...The still, sad music of humanity,

Nor harsh nor grating, though of ample power
To chasten and subdue...
...a sense sublime   'Tintern Abbey', 1798.
Of something far more deeply interfused,
Whose dwelling is the light of setting suns,
And the round sea and the living air,
And the blue sky and in the mind of man.

Coleridge's view of Freedom breaking a 'triple chain' and the freed peasant living and 'no fetter vile the mind shall know' ('The Destruction of the Bastille') is language that clearly recalls Blake's 'mind forged manacles' ('London', *Songs of Experience*). As human beings, both Blake and Coleridge are concerned with the future of society, but as writers it is the workings of the human mind and imagination that occupies them. No wonder one of the things Coleridge looks forward to is the 'fearless glow' of 'Eloquence'.

5

The visual arts

The Raft of the Medusa

Taught by a follower of David, Théodore Géricault (1791–1824) was only in his late twenties when he painted what was to become not only his most famous work, but also one of the most famous expressions of Romanticism in the visual arts. *The Raft of the Medusa* (1819) told a story, and a real one at that: the ship sank, the wave-tossed survivors clung to a raft, the newspapers of the day carried accounts of what had happened.

For more on David, see page 49.

Géricault had chosen a subject which gave him the opportunity to imitate the works of Caravaggio and Michelangelo, all straining bodies and dramatically expressive faces. *The Raft of the Medusa* draws on the inheritance of the Deposition and Entombment of Christ, as can be seen in his calculated endebtedness to the struggling knots of people painted by Rubens and Rembrandt. Géricault takes this explicitly religious form and applies it to a secular event, yet knows that the implicit tradition will evoke in the viewer a certain response. Thus human suffering is sacramentalised, just as Nature, in the poetry of Wordsworth, is infused with the Holy Spirit as if after its own Pentecost. For an example of a landscape acquiring sacramental status in the visual arts, look at Friedrich's painting *Morgen im Riesengebirge*. This depicts a crucifixion, but the background has seized control of the painting to such an extent that the painting communicates itself as secular rather than religious art. The very title tells us that the subject matter is a morning scene in the Sudeten mountains, as if the crucifixion is there simply to confirm that the value systems in art have been overturned.

In addition, the positioning of the figures in *The Raft of the Medusa* resembles that of the political icons of the French Revolution, the waving of the shirt recalling the raising of the tricolour. But who is that at the apex of the triangle of struggling bodies? It is a black man. This figure, the highest representative of human suffering and hope, is fulfilling several important functions. His prominence:

The tricolour motif was also picked up by Delacroix in *Liberty Leading the People*, 1830.

- Reminds the viewer that the disaster took place off the west African coast
- Contributes to the debate of whether freedom is divisible (as in the case of Toussaint)
- Feeds the Romantic fascination with Africa
- Evokes Géricault's inheritance from Baroque artists such as Rubens, who painted out of delight in the human form and fascination for familiar muscles seen in an unfamiliar skin.

The subject of a wreck allows Géricault to depict a seascape, a Romantic subject he shares with Turner and Casper David Friedrich (as we shall see on page 52). The result is a painting of human destiny: we must expect to be the victims of a hostile universe; we have to assume that danger, shipwreck, starvation and violence will come our way. As a composition it recalls the structure of Romantic symphonies: the heroic struggles of the opening movement and the funeral march that sometimes occurs in the adagio that follows. Géricault has simply omitted the scherzo and the final triumph of the last movement, which so often contains a march. In doing so he reflects the mood of his times: France has lost Napoleon and the revolutionary wars. On the throne was the ultra-conservative Charles X of the restored Bourbons and the 1816 disaster was interpreted (especially by the anti-Bourbon newspaper which broke the story) as the consequence of their incompetent leadership. He is also reflecting the true details of the story. We see the uppermost survivor seeking to attract the attention of a ship far off on the horizon. Survivors described how this ship in fact disappeared from view, prompting several passengers to commit suicide, before reappearing and carrying out the rescue.

> Charles X was restored twice over: once following the abdication of Napoleon in 1814 and again after his defeat at Waterloo in 1815.

Nature: friend or foe?

We should note the contrast between Nature, as portrayed by Géricault, and Nature as described by Mendelssohn and Schumann. In the latter, Nature is supportive and embracing; it is our natural home and we belong there. The sea in Mendelssohn's *Calm Sea and Prosperous Voyage* and the river in Schumann's Symphony No 3 are closer to the world of Friedrich's *Monk on a Seashore* and *Der Wanderer über dem Nebelmeer* (see below, page 51) than to Géricault's Atlantic. In the *Medusa*, humanity is dramatically alone in a hostile landscape. To provide a point of contrast, let us turn to Classical landscape works such as Gainsborough's *Mr and Mrs Andrews* and Raeburn's *Reverend Robert Walker Skating on Duddingston Loch*. The individuals portrayed by these paintings are:

- Engaged in a leisure activity: Nature is relaxing
- In a landscape which, though not domesticated, is nevertheless tame and close to the human-ordered, George Knightley-approved world of towns and farms: Nature is safe
- Smartly dressed, down to their hats and gloves: Nature is polite
- Going nowhere: Nature is stable
- At home in their surroundings: Nature is owned.

And so these paintings are also, implicitly, about human nature: they teach us that people are relaxing, safe, polite and stable, a position which certainly resonates with the Classical period's Enlightenment lesson. More than that, the fact that one painting shows a man taking a book into the countryside teaches us that human culture and Nature belong together: civilisation and culture come naturally to us and are not (as Jean Jacques Rousseau had argued) an imposition or acquisition. The late 17th- and 18th-century arts comfortably embrace Nature. We can:

- Hear this in Handel's 'Pastoral Symphony' (*Messiah*, Act 1)
- Read this in Thomson's *The Seasons*
- See this in Claude's landscapes, with their Classical architecture set among smooth lawns and pleasantly arranged trees.

In contrast to Classicism's confidence in the concord of God's world with human reason, Géricault, Delacroix and Friedrich all accept Nature as a challenge to the individual, who must accept struggle and loneliness. However, in Casper David Friedrich Nature is not actively out to crush the hero, as it appears to be in Géricault. The German painter's Nature appears designed to inspire us to new heights of achievement. Similarly, Schumann's landscapes may involve rivers and storms, but these are optimistic forces because they are evidence of natural energy and confidence, and not merely threats. Mendelssohn's blustery sea is the source of mercantile prosperity: the threat is not from a menacing Géricault-style storm but from a calm sea, because the ships that bring middle-class profits are then unable to move. Friedrich's *Monk on a Seashore* recalls Baudelaire's *L'Homme et la Mer* (Man and the Sea), with its declaration:

> La mer est ton miroir; tu contemples ton âme
> Dans le déroulement infini de sa lame…
> Homme, nul n'a sondé le fond de tes abîmes.

> The sea is your mirror; you contemplate your soul
> In the endless unfurling of its waves...
> Humanity, no one has probed your depths in full.

Géricault is more the heir to the philosophy of struggle and conflict inherent in David's calmly structured painting of the *Death of Marat* and *Oath of the Horatii* than he may at first appear. Indeed, Géricault himself called David the *régénerateur* (regenerator) of French painting, and Delacroix acknowledged him as the *père* (father) of the modern school. David, after all, was the creator of the Napoleonic myth in art and, in his painting of the *Marat Assassiné*, established the right of art to comment on current events, something both Géricault and Delacroix went on to do.

See Walter Friedlaender, *David to Delacroix* (originally *Von David bis Delacroix*, 1930; translated and various reprints).

Delacroix

In the same way that Géricault saw himself as the heir to Michelangelo and Caravaggio, so Eugène Delacroix (1798–1863) revered Correggio, Michelangelo, Raphael and Titian. Like Géricault, Delacroix established himself early on as a man to watch, quickly becoming a major player in the debate surrounding the nature of Romanticism and the future of art. His contemporary Ingrès (1780–1867) submitted his pious *Vow of Louis XIII* at the same time as Delacroix his *Massacre* at *Chios* (*Scènes des massacres de Scio*, Louvre, Paris). Ingrès was a Romantic in one sense of the word, as he, like Walter Scott before him, chose a medieval subject. Delacroix was also a Romantic, but of a different ilk, as demonstrated by his use of art to report on current events (in this case the news of a war crime in the Greek War of Independence, the same war in which Byron died). Critics complained that the painting was all despair and destruction, asking where were the patriots vowing revenge, as in David's revered *Oath of the Horatii*? Just as Géricault invokes the Deposition, does Delacroix expect us to recall the Massacre of Innocents in this painting?

Constable

The modern Briton is used to seeing his country as the home of Shakespeare and Newton, at the forefront of literature and science, but a backwater for music and the visual arts. Thus it is perhaps hard for us to grasp the fact that we can lay claim to some great masters in both these fields, and John Constable (1776–1837) is certainly one. The Royal Academy famously requested the removal of his *Water Meadows Near Salisbury*, calling it a 'nasty green thing': but what does this tale teach us? The son of a Suffolk mill owner, Constable himself said that a carefree rural boyhood on the banks of the Stour had made him a painter. It certainly

> *Constable*, John Sunderland, Phaidon, is short, affordable and illustrated.

helped make him a precise observer of the natural world just at a time when such a precision on this subject was about to come into high fashion. But we should fight shy of dubbing Constable a 'landscape painter'; for one thing, note that his painting never made him a tourist. He rarely moved far from his native country, and this is of more than mere biographical interest. A tour to the English Lake District, a visit to Salisbury and a view of Hadleigh Castle are among the few departures which he undertook with paintbrush in hand. In painting Suffolk landscapes, Constable was painting something he knew intimately: like Baudelaire writing about Paris and Wordsworth about childhood, and like Berlioz composing the *Symphonie fantastique*, his was autobiographical art. The *Boat-Building near Flatford*, *Haywain*, *Leaping Horse*, *Stratford Mill*, *View near the Stour, near Dedham*, *White Horse* and *Chain Peer, Brighton* all show places he knew as a child. He sets out to paint not merely verisimilitude, but truth.

In the case of *The Haywain* (1821), the modern title points the viewer to the wagon which appears to be going nowhere. The title under which it was exhibited, *Landscape: Noon,* at least has the virtue of attracting the viewer's attention to the study of light and place, human life and natural rhythms. For the clouds, the man fishing and the low-flying swallows, the young woman washing laundry and the haymakers in the field all tell a story of the time of year, the time of day and the kind of weather to be expected. The signature on the work tells us that the painter was in London, and we know that he wrote to consult a friend concerning details of the hay cart. Like Wordsworth, he was recollecting emotion in tranquillity.

Constable's success in his home country was limited: his friends bought his work, the public largely ignored him and the Royal Academy snubbed him even when it finally elected him to membership. In France, he was what the art world had been waiting for and, as noted above, both Géricault and Delacroix admired him. He has only finally become famous in Britain now that he has lost

In this respect, Constable is similar to Elgar, who was once hailed by Strauss as Britain's great Modernist composer.

the moniker of a Romantic and has instead become associated with 'Nostalgic' art, a movement on which Britain is particularly keen, and where his work rubs shoulders with the *Forsyte Saga* and the operettas of Gilbert and Sullivan. But paintings which offer modern Britain the appeal of old-fashioned clothes and traditional farming were, at the beginning of the 19th century, examples of a revolutionary art. The famous 'green thing' comment resonates with the sort of abuse works such as Schoenberg's *Verklärte Nacht* received at the other end of the century.

Landscape painting had previously been subject to the same level of 'improvement' as landscape gardening. Painters had rearranged the phenomena as required to make a pleasant arrangement on the canvas, as one would in a still life. When Constable paints, he is doing much what Samuel Johnson did

Admittedly, even Constable has been shown to be not entirely free of 'improvement' of nature in his painting.

when he kicked a stone to refute philosopher Bishop Berkley (and when Bertrand Russell referred to physical reality as a 'brute fact'). He is accepting physical reality on a metaphysical level. As a Romantic, he is painting Nature as a way of defining human nature: this is our home, this is where we belong and this is who we are. Even his dedicated studies of cloud formations have an implicit visionary quality. A hundred years later, the evidently visionary nature of William Blake's art (finally) attracted Symbolist and Modernist attentions. We do Constable wrong if we fail to acknowledge his Romantic achievement.

Friedrich

Caspar David Friedrich (1774–1840) was perhaps a more consciously literary, or symbolic, painter than Delacroix and Géricault. Like them he painted landscapes, but he tended to include elements from a recognisable iconography: the ruins of some ecclesiastical buildings point to the transience of human life and the ravages time wreaks on all human achievements. In this respect, his work echoes the Medieval and Renaissance tradition of setting the Nativity in a ruined noble building to symbolise the beginnings of the Church alongside the ruins of Judaism.

Another key element in Friedrich's visual vocabulary is mist. The hiker in *Der Wanderer über dem Nebelmeer* has cloud swirling around his feet. As a technical phenomenon, Friedrich's mists impress the viewer by obscuring the usual clarity concerning foreground, figures, depth, setting and the like. As a philosophical contribution, it challenges Classicism's confidence by questioning whether either we or our world are finally knowable. After all, Classicism as a philosophical standpoint had been founded on Enlightenment science, with its emphasis on rigorous observation. Friedrich himself participates in this by sketching careful studies of plants, rocks and trees. But the swirls of mist and the sea spray that confront his monk on the seashore undermine the ontological confidence that we truly can observe and record. Although Constable did not privilege mist as Friedrich did, he did make preparatory scientific studies of nature. In his case, the fascination was with clouds. Clouds are fascinating because of their constant mobility and fluidity.

Clouds were an obscurity, like mist and fog, but they were also a symbol of human destiny, in the way that they are blown and buffeted by the wind, choosing neither their own shape nor their direction. This indeterminacy is what Wordsworth had in mind in the *Daffodills* poem cited earlier. Its opening, in which the author describes how he had come upon the flowers at the edge of a lake while wandering 'lonely as a cloud' is in part a statement of the nature of human destiny See page 35. and in part a discussion of poetic inspiration. In the passage from his *Ode: Intimations of Immortality* already quoted, the 'clouds of glory' are spiritual, fragments of the soul that predate our birth and will outlive our time in this world.

James Mallord William **Turner** (1775–1851), like Constable, admired Claude. Almost exact contemporaries, these two great English Romantics have a great deal in common, although Turner's works are perhaps more similar to those of European Romantics. For one thing, his painting of *Staffa: Fingal's Cave* is bound to strike a chord with students of music. His painting of a snowstorm entitled *Hannibal Crossing the Alps* has an appeal to history that several French poets, their interest in classical history ignited by the Napoleonic experience, would understand. To call him a 'nature painter' is as misleading as it would be to call Constable a landscape painter. One snowstorm painting shows us Hannibal, but another shows a steamboat at a harbour mouth: the former evokes history and the heroic; the latter industry, commerce and business as usual.

Two schools?

Here we see two separate wings of Romanticism emerge: for some the truth about human nature lies in the titanic and dramatic, for others it is to be found in the humdrum and everyday. The implicit conflict between these interpretations confuses our understanding of the movement even now. Romanticism spawned **Realism** and **Naturalism**, the painting of Jean-François Millet and Gustave Courbet. But from the same wellspring of enquiry came the **Symbolists** such as Odilon Redon and Gustave Moreau, with their Baudelaire-influenced concern to find the arcane, even occult truth about our true nature (see page 58).

Trying to see these conflicting schools as equal expressions of Romanticism may appear counterintuitive, but a closer look at the full range of Gauguin and Van Gogh, and the work of the Pre-Raphaelites, will tell its own story. Van Gogh's *Potato Eaters* is fundamentally a sympathetic (socialist) portrait of poverty. Ford

Madox Brown's *Work* is everything that Biedermeier's social paintings fail to be: a dramatic situation in which different social classes are going about their different business, sharing a townscape, living alongside one another yet clearly isolated from each other. The work betrays no sentimentality or pathos: the working men work, the rich own possessions, the artists look on and observe. The work of the title is clearly disruptive, and the town and society are being forced to confront change, but whether this is a positive or negative development remains unclear. This is obviously not a religious work in the way Holman Hunt's paintings such as *The Light of the World* and *The Scapegoat* are, but the organisation of the painting clearly owes a debt to late medieval religious art, such as the Van Eyck brothers' *Adoration of the Lamb*, which demonstrates their ability to organise complex designs in which several scenarios interact.

Turner may be popularly associated with seascapes to match Constable's landscapes, but he also painted *Ulysses Deriding Polyphemus* and *Dido Building Carthage*, subjects taken from Latin and Greek literature, in the same way that Shelley (*Prometheus Unbound*) and José-Maria de Hérédia (*Antoine et Cléopatre*) adopt subjects from antiquity in their poetry. To match this exploration of history and literature, Turner toured in search of material, travelling through France, Germany and Italy. Like Constable, he gradually defined his experiment: in his case it focused on light and colour. It is tempting to see the contrast between the stay-at-home Constable and the restless Turner as indicative of two contrasting schools of Romanticism, for if Constable is depicting nature as a haven and a home (as Wordsworth did), Turner is depicting it as a hostile, challenging force, as Byron did in his poetry and Géricault did in his seascapes.

A brave new world

We find this sense of awe at the power implicit in a landscape in paintings such as *Buttermere Lake, with Part of Cromackwater, Cumberland, a Shower*, which Turner painted about the time Wordsworth was writing the 'Lucy' poems, and shortly before he moved to the Lake District. Like Wordsworth, Turner travelled to the Alps, and as Wordsworth wrote about the crossing in Book 6 of *The Prelude*, so Turner painted the Riechenback Falls, the St Gothard Pass, and a study of an avalanche destroying a cottage.

Thirty five years before he wrote his analysis of the French Revolution, Edmund Burke had published a study of aesthetics in which he contrasted the concept of beauty with that of the sublime. With a word deriving from Classical literary theory (specifically Longinus), he made a distinction between beautiful things that induce pleasure and sublime things that induce awe:

Edmund Burke, *A Philosophical Enquiry into the Origin of Our Ideas of the Sublime and Beautiful*, 1757.

> *Whatever is in any sort terrible or is conversant about terrible objects or operates in a manner analogous to terror, is a source of the Sublime.*

It has not been shown that Turner himself had read Burke, but the work was so widespread in its influence on taste, that it would have been difficult for him not to have been aware of its content.

It would, however, be a mistake to limit our understanding of Turner's achievement to a modern idea of the natural. This was a time of industrialisation and in his *Rain, Steam and Speed*, the power of a storm and that of a steam train are depicted on the same canvas. This is a world away from the railway paintings of Biedermeier artists, with their reassuring depiction of people sensibly going about the business of travel in a modest celebration of human technical achievement. Turner shows the twin dramas of the natural and the manufactured. This is a very different landscape from those painted by Gainsborourgh (and farmed by George Knightley and his tenant Robert Martin: *Emma*). That had been a world in which Nature cooperated with human beings and was ordered by them, where horses waited patiently in harness and the harvest wagon filled up. By contrast, Turner's painting celebrates a power that cannot be mastered, but which human beings, represented in this case by Great Western Railways, were now seeking, like Victor Frankenstein, to imitate.

Should we think less of Constable, that he seems to have eschewed railways and factories? Some have attacked his art, as they have that of Jane Austen, for making less of developments than contemporaries such as Turner and Scott. Certainly he does not fill his landscapes with the wounded of the Napoleonic wars, nor does he show ruffian gangs of demobilised soldiers performing robberies. There is no sign of the 1816 failure of the harvest. There are not even the gypsies who frighten Harriet Smith (*Emma*). He remains loyal not to what is new, but to what has resisted change.

In Turner's *Fighting Temeraire* (1838) we can see two sides of the same coin. Dominating the composition is a large old-style sailing ship of the line, a veteran of several naval encounters, perhaps a hero of the Napoleonic wars. But dominating the Temeraire itself is a small tug boat, what John Masefield might have called a 'dirty British' working ship, powered by coal. The painting's full title explains that the sailing ship is being 'tugged to her last berth' and is to be dismantled. The contrast between heroic and commercial, past and present, is staring us in the face, but if we have too fixed an idea about what is Romantic, defining Turner as a 'nature' or 'seascape' painter, we won't see the contrast (we may not even see the tug). This contrast is part of what helped create the Impressionism that is late Romanticism's great achievement in art, and which in turn helped create Modernism.

The Nostalgia school of art appreciation sees in the art of the late Romantics and Impressionists only pretty fields and women in old-fashioned frocks. This tunnel vision is created in part by the extent of change that we have witnessed in the nature of the landscape over the last hundred years. Painters from Turner to Utrillo were showing us what were, at the time, novelties: the Temeraire's tug, railways and steam trains, and the newly laid-out streets of Norwood. To a contemporary observer, these innovations have acquired a patina of age; they have become the very tradition that they once threatened. When Tennyson and

Superveille wrote about the railways (and they were unusual in doing so, since much 19th-century poetry ignored large swathes of human experience), they were examining something new: in the case of Tennyson, new to society, and even for Superveille, still new to poetry. Yet the French poet's celebration of transcontinental expresses now exists in a startlingly different context: those trains themselves seem almost as old as the knights in armour adored by Weber and painted by Rossetti, such is the speed of technological change. The luxury trains are part of a lost world of monarchies destroyed by two world wars. All this makes it hard for us to see the upheaval inherent in Romantic art.

> While Beethoven is still modern and Schoenberg cutting edge, technology more than 20 years old can seem antique.

Edgar Degas (1834–1917) knew better. This painter of race horses and ballet dancers, and friend of Renoir, declared shrewdly that 'If I were the government I would have a company of police watching out for men who paint landscapes from nature'. This can only confirm our impression that socialism was yet another child of Romanticism.

6
The legacy of Romanticism

Reality and its symbols

During the course of the 19th century, Romanticism split into two distinct camps. The first consisted of writers whose concern with man's place in society led them to work within the conventions of realist fiction. The second group, however, distanced themselves from the material reality of life, instead pursuing Romanticism's fascination with the mystical and

These realist conventions were set out, often conflictingly, by 18th-century writers such as Richardson, Fielding and Smollett, and parodied by Sterne.

the occult. By picking up on different aspects of Romanticism, the paths of the Realists, Naturalists and Biedermeier artists on one hand, and the Symbolists and Pre-Raphaelites on the other, diverged significantly.

Influenced by developments in scientific thought, the **Realism** of Balzac and Flaubert led to **Naturalism**, as writers such as Zola and Ibsen took an often scientific approach to the study of individuals, families and societies. Zola's 20-novel study of life in Second Empire France explores genetics and the heredity of character.

In painting, Courbet's realism leads straight to the social observations of painters such as James Tissot (*The Gallery of H.M.S. 'Calcutta' (Portsmouth)*, *Gentleman in a Railway Carriage*), William Powell Frith (*The Railway Station*) and Abraham Solomon (*First Class*). Why all the railway settings? Firstly, because they are places of social interaction, allowing the artist to enjoy the coincidence of characters. Secondly, they are modern and in fashion, while also bringing the social agenda to the fore (just as factories and streets are foregrounded in industrial novels).

But are these works examples of complacent Biedermeier or grittier Naturalism? The distinction is in the treatment. The Naturalism of Ibsen and Zola shows the human animal, capable both of heroism and of savagery, and society as a whole. The title of Zola's novel, *La Bête humaine*, another work with a railway setting, was not chosen at random. The Biedermeier artist in any medium shows charm and treats his subjects with a reassuring smile. Perhaps this indirectly explains why Baudelaire was as unenthusiastic about Courbet, as he was about photography: art was not merely a matter of making tidy copies. By contrast, he declared of Manet, whom like Mallarmé he did admire, that he was capable of revealing the hidden epic within the everyday. Tissot, Frith and Solomon are Biedermeier, convinced that different social

Linda Nochlin, *Realism and Tradition in Art 1848–1900*, London: Pelican.

classes are kept at a safe difference. Compare Solomon's *First Class* and *Third Class*: these show different worlds and are even painted in a different style; for the working class, he shifts into a cartoon style suitable for *Punch*.

The woman question

Later, Ibsen's plays *The Doll's House* and *Hedda Gabler* ask not so much *what is man?* as *what is woman?*. This more modern take on the self debate can also be found in German literature, most notably in *Effi Briest* (1895), Fontane's examination of the constraints facing women in Wilhelmine society. In English, Hardy's *Tess of the d'Urbervilles* similarly shows a woman responding to her destiny and demonstrating the heroic strengths and weaknesses of her character.

> The influence of Shakespeare, Scott and Thackeray can be keenly felt in Fontane's work, and in her formative years, the eponymous Effi reads *David Copperfield*, which itself is a tale of growing up.

To what effect though? Was it merely a case of Romanticism adapting itself? The importance of 'woman' both in realist and symbolic art is an important one, providing a linking function between apparently disparate late-Romantic schools. As written about or painted by men, she is variously muse, stranger, outsider, foreigner and threat, yet also true human nature, a kind of noble savage. She can also represent the modern world, with the rise of the so-called 'woman question'. There is thus a link between the heroine on Keats' Greek urn, Baudelaire's whores and lesbians, Hedda Gabler, Emma Bovary, Effi Briest, Tess, Salammbô, Dora (Spenlow) Copperfield, Agnes Wickfield and Estella (Havisham).

The theme of prostitution in particular bridged the two schools of late Romanticism. On the one hand, it presents human beings in extreme situations. It connects with the theme of adultery and exclusion from society that we see in *Effi Briest*, *Tess of the d'Urbervilles* and *Madame Bovary*. In Marxist terms prostitution lays bare the true economic nature of bourgeois relationships – including marriage – between men and women. We find it outside the realm of fiction in the autobiographical *Confessions of an English Opium Eater* (1822) by Coleridge's friend Thomas de Quincey. This describes the similarities between the author and a prostitute: they are both in their teens and both half starving. Critics often contrast their presentation in Balzac and that in Hugo.

The prostitute in Romantic literature also links into the theme of woman as threat and develops it even beyond the caricature of bourgeois acquisitiveness Balzac depicted. The theme of vampirism is significant in Baudelaire: the character addressed in 'Le Vampire' is an 'Infâme à qui je suis lié / Comme le forçat à la chaîne'. 'Les Métamorphoses du vampire' describes the woman as apparently flushed with blood (her

> Translation: 'Abomination to which I am tied/ Like the convict to the chain.'

mouth is red and damp), but reveals her at the end of the poem to be little more than bones. Like de Quincey, he equates the creative artist with the prostitute: in 'Les Foules', art is a 'sainte prostitution' ('sacred prostitution').

This unifying theme aside, many important writers did cross the divide between the two late-Romantic schools. Flaubert wrote the realist masterpiece *Madame Bovary* and belonged to a firmly anti-Biedermeier wing of Realism: for him private life was not a refuge but the place where public policy was tested and (reminiscent of Austen's view of courtship), the crucible where human nature was judged. However, he is also the novelist who went in search of the exotic. This can be seen in *La Tentation de Saint Antoine*, *Salammbô*, *Herodiade* and *La Légende de Saint Julien l'Hospitalier*, with their New Testament, Carthaginian and Medieval subjects and settings. It is also important not to neglect the way in which Flaubert is an ironist (a word that first comes into literary discussion with the early German Romantic theorists): Emma Bovary's character and destiny are formed to some degree by her consumption of Romantic novels.

Arthur Rimbaud's 'Le Mal' to some extent anticipates the realist style of First World War poetry, while his 'Le Dormeur du val' (creatively translated by Robert Lowell in *Imitations*) is not unlike the Wilfred Owen poem 'Move him into the sun' (set by Britten in the *War Requiem*). But despite his tender treatment of death ('Le Dormeur du val') and sensuality ('Rêvé pour l'hiver'), he, like Flaubert, sought out the exotic, studying the occult and seeking out tobacco, alcohol, hashish and sexual experience. His explanation of the making of a poet reflects this: 'Le Poëte se fait voyant par un longue, immense et raisonné *dérèglement de tous les sens*.' Note the defiant use of the word 'raisonné' there! This may to some degree recall the Coleridge of *Kubla Khan*, but is a long way from Wordsworth's emotion recollected in tranquillity.

> Translation: 'The poet gains his insight by embarking on a long, grand and calculated *derailment of all his senses*.' (Italics Rimbaud's own.)

Oscar Wilde specialised in pretending to be a Biedermeier playwright, offering light comedies about the upper middle classes, while undermining that same social group's self-assurance. These nods to Biedermeier Realism aside, Wilde was deeply influenced by 19th-century French literature: his *Salomé* was indeed written in French (and under the influence of Symbolist art; think of Moreau) and turned into an opera by Richard Strauss. He was accordingly parodied as part of the late-Romantic aesthetic movement by those triumphs of English Biedermeier theatre, Gilbert and Sullivan (*Patience*).

> Wilde's contemporary and fellow countryman Shaw adopted a similar pose and approach, albeit one reflecting the styles of different decades, for Shaw started writing plays more or less as Wilde ceased.

The **Pre-Raphaelites** and the **Symbolists** form the other side of the post-Romantic coin. These schools picked up on quite a different aspect of late Romanticism to their Realist and Naturalist contemporaries, striving to find the arcane, even occult truth about our world and our true nature. Aestheticism itself traces its ancestry to Keats' elevation of Beauty to a moral as well as aesthetic plane (*Ode on a Grecian Urn*); there is something Keatsian (subtly different from the Byronic) about its insistence on intensity.

The inward-looking, increasingly self-reflexive aspect of early Romanticism led to the Keatsian poetry of Tennyson, and in France to Mallarmé's examination of the nature of poetic communication. Mallarmé was indeed an admirer of Tennyson, as he was of Poe. It is true that Tennyson tries to respond to contemporary concerns. His *The Princess* examines the 'woman question'; *Loxley Hall* investigates territory Elizabeth Gaskell would recognise. But the awkward balancing act he has to perform in handling the competing groups in that narration indicates the extent to which Tennyson was not at ease with the task. He seems not to want to approve either the conservatives or the radicals on the question, and opts instead for a Biedermeier tone: his conclusion appears to be that things which don't matter must change in order for those things that do to stay the same.

> English Literature 1832–1890
> Excluding the Novel, Paul Turner,
> OUP 1989, pages 18–38.

Music

Literature continued to exercise its influence over music. Strauss may have been a torchbearer for Modernism in his youth, but that did not prevent him from being a late-Romantic composer as well, writing a *Macbeth* tone poem in the 1880s. However, with the advent of Nationalism, Romanticism achieved the unexpected, which was the balkanisation of classical music. Of course, Baroque music had known Italian and French styles, but German composers were equally adept at both. Under later Romanticism, however, it became the done thing for composers to seek out the indigenous style of their native land. Thus in Russia, Glinka became the father of his country's music, as Smetana was in his native Bohemia. Polish, Hungarian and Scottish composers also set out to define a national sound. Any country which

> Poetry saw similar developments, with Pushkin in Russia and Mickiewicz in Poland.

belonged to the Austro-Hungarian empire felt that a composer should be able to demonstrate the ways in which he was independent of the Austrian classical tradition.

No opera, audiences must have felt, was now complete without peasants dancing in national costume, preferably to a regional dance tune or rhythm. Chopin and the Polonaise, Liszt and his Hungarian rhapsodies, Dvořák and his Slavonic rhapsodies all point to an awareness of local

> An example of this is Smetana's opera, *The Bartered Bride*.

loyalty. Later on, England enjoyed an 'English Rhapsody' (Delius' *Brigg Fair*) and a *Norfolk Rhapsody* (Vaughan Williams), while Enescu wrote two Romanian Rhapsodies which all contained echoes of folk songs. Grieg (Norway), Albéniz, Falla and Granados (Spain) and Sibelius (Finland) all produced late Romantic music with regional qualities, a Hispanic harmony here or a Hungarian triplet there. In America, the visiting Dvořák's announcement that the local idiom was to be found in African-American music did not delight all his hosts, but it did turn out to be prophetic, certainly as far as popular music was concerned.

I have already pointed to Mahler's and Elgar's first symphonies as late examples of Romantic programme music. There is, for example,

> These were composed in 1884 and 1908 respectively.

something about the A♭ first subject of Elgar's Andante which is fatefully march-like (tellingly marked *Nobilmente*), while the Scherzo offers both a $\frac{2}{2}$ march and a distinctly pastoral interlude. Similarly, to create a warm countryside for his faune in *Prélude à 'L'Après midi d'un faune'*, Debussy draws on the pastoral sounds of the flute, oboe and horn.

The insistence of Constable on the continuing landscape of his boyhood in the face of social and economic change is to be found in another form in the art of the Pre-Raphaelites and the Arts and Crafts Movement, which responded to industrialisation by seeking to revalidate traditional skills and by extension the value of a human being and his creativity. William Morris figures in both of these developments – and in the story of the development of the socialist movement in Britain, reminding us again of Degas' observation.

Later still, Shostakovich's allegedly penitent Symphony No 5 is a marvellous example of the fact that he understood, far better than the authorities, what Romanticism really meant. The composer himself revealed that the concealed programme in the fifth was the same as that of the fourth (which was withdrawn by the composer), namely the suffering of the Stalinist interwar purges. He deliberately avoided a triumphant finale, he declared in his autobiographical *Testimony*, since exultation could not be justified in the Soviet Union of the 1930s.

> It is important to acknowledge that the authenticity of these memoirs, said to have been written by Solomon Volkov but based on a series of interviews, has been questioned.

His Symphony No 4 ended with a faintly Mahlerian funeral march, interrupted by a threatening passage in which we are hustled along. Symphony No 5 has a slow-paced grieving third movement in which the brass are silent, making the opening of the finale, with its stamping timpani and roaring winds, suggest violent celebration. It is almost as if the orchestra are celebrating while being beaten, something the composer himself suggested. Yet the quotation from one of his own songs, *Rebirth,* is enough to suggest that behind the falsity of official festivals, there is genuine reason to retain hope. On hearing the piece Khrennikov (a party-liner, pedestrian composer and denouncer of geniuses) was suspicious that there was more to it than met the ear, but was insufficiently astute to track down the true anti-Soviet programme. According to the party line, a Romantic work was long and loud, with a large brass section to make the state and its leaders feel important. Shostakovich, however, realised that a Romantic work was an enquiry into humanity and a personal statement. To them the 1937 symphony was an apology; to its composer it was an affirmation.

7
Further perspectives

Romanticism is a large subject; this is a small book. My purpose here was to examine an idea, not to analyse a selection of symphonies, novels or paintings. In fact I could have chosen a rather different range of creative artists to illustrate the same points and conduct the same argument. It is, however, important to note that many important writers, painters and composers have been omitted from this book or have not been given the treatment they deserve.

Literature
The following suggestions for further reading should complement your understanding of English, German and French Romantic literature respectively.

- Browning's poetry and plays
- Gaskell's *Wives and Daughters*
- Oliphant's *Mrs Marjoribanks*
- Eliot's *Middlemarch*
- Keats' *Ode on a Grecian Urn*
- Tennyson (although note he later went out of fashion and is today viewed as an exponent not of Romantic but of Victorian literature)
- Scott: start with *Waverley* and stick to the novels he set in Scotland
- Arnold's small poetic and larger prose œuvre, especially *Dover Beach* and *Culture and Anarchy*
- Peacock's *Nightmare Abbey*, a comic gothic novel in which a pseudonymous Shelley is one of the characters.

- The philosopher Kant (start with Körner's short introduction)
- Kleist (*Prinz Friedrich von Homburg* and *Die Marquise von O*)
- Novalis (*Hymnen an die Nacht*)
- Jean Paul (who described the human unconscious as an inner Africa waiting to be explored)
- The Schlegel brothers (who translated Shakespeare)
- Hoffman (who took the Romantic theme of the bizarre into far darker, more menacing territory).

Non-Germanists could start with a small anthology like the *Penguin Book of German Verse* (ed. Forster), which has the benefit of accompanying prose translations.

- The philosopher Jean Jacques Rousseau
- Stendhal (*Le Rouge et le Noir, La Chartreuse de Parme*)
- Victor Hugo (start with the well-known *Notre-Dame de Paris* but also read his astounding poetry, which is often neglected by British readers)

- Baudelaire's *Les Fleurs du Mal*
- Rimbaud's verse and his prose poetry *Illuminations*.

Visual arts

The following avenues of enquiry would reward further study:

- 19th-century genre painting (pictures that tell a story). Leading exponents are the Scot David Wilkie and his Irish contemporary William Mulready. Some of their paintings respond directly to the Jacobite legends established in Walter Scott's fiction.
- Romantic sculpture, especially that of Degas and Rodin.
- A comparison of the German 'Nazarene' artists of the Brotherhood of St Luke (formed in 1809) and the Pre-Raphaelite Brotherhood.

  > The Nazarene artists were dedicated to imitating pre-Renaissance art, a protest against stultifying academic rigidity.

- Impressionism: start with the transitional figure, Manet, and trace the movement's development through Monet, Sisley and the arguably Biedermeier Renoir, to the post-Impressionism of Van Gogh and Cézanne.
- *Art pour l'art* and the ivory tower. Investigate further the terms Parnassianism, Aestheticism, Decadence and Symbolism.

Music

As the music chapter concentrated more on early Romanticism, the following composers would provide good starting points for an investigation of late Romantic music.

- Wagner: his overture to *Tannhäuser* and *Siegfried Idyll* are good places to start, and *Das Rheingold* is both musically and dramatically exciting.
- Puccini: *La bohème* is touching and powerful, and reflects the Romantic movement's own debate on the lifestyle of the creative artist (see page 5). His work has long enjoyed popular success, but musicologists have also enjoyed analysing his use of motifs and his treatment of women (they tend to suffer and die).
- Rachmaninov: the *Rococo Variations* for cello and the Symphony No 1 are both immediately attractive and the composer wrote a wealth of work for piano, mostly for his own performance.
- Sibelius: *Finlandia* and the violin concerto are enduringly popular, and he also wrote a series of symphonies and tone poems culminating in *Tapiola*.
- Nielson: his Symphony No 4, the *Inextinguishable*, was written in the aftermath of the First World War. His Symphony No 5 is famous for its prominent use of the snare drum.

It would however be a mistake to believe that Romantic works are always on a Gargantuan scale: for examples of more subtle Romantic music listen to Smetana's string quartets, and the songs of Wolf, Mahler and Vaughan Williams.

Conclusion

In the field of popular entertainment, fiction, music, films and even journalism continue to be written according to Romantic aesthetic principles, and to express a Romantic code of values. The theme of falling in love, which came to dominate the fiction of the Romantic century, eventually subsumed the term entirely, and if the demand for romantic entertainment is worryingly insatiable, so the supply of novels and films that feed it is comfortingly inexhaustible.

Film plots regularly enact the Romantic code. Popular novels and their film adaptations include a large number of relationship plots, but also a great deal of detective (and science) fiction is directly endebted to Romanticism, even when it is not, like *Gone with the Wind* and *Rebecca*, modelled on existing works. Detective fiction and films are indeed part of Romanticism's legacy, with their insistence that life needs examining, and their understanding of more shadowy aspects of humanity. Gothic principles may have fallen out of fashion in literary fiction a long time ago, but their popularity in film has recently succeeded in restoring the genre.

The first composers of film music grew up during the Romantic era, and, to this day, film music frequently adheres to Romanticism's harmonic rules. There is much to enjoy in the soundtracks of earlier composers such as Erich Korngold (*Adventures of Robin Hood*), Franz Waxman (*Rebecca*) and Max Steiner (*Gone with the Wind*), and later ones such as John Williams.

Romanticism was perhaps the most successful upheaval in the arts ever, and like many a protest movement, the revolutionaries eventually found themselves in government. As a result, what had been radical became conventional, the revolutionary became academic, and thus the achievement of genius became codified so that others could imitate it. Sometimes this means that we have lost our sense of how dangerous Romantic works were. The extent to which the artistic establishment had forgotten what Romanticism truly stood for was shown by how many masterpieces of Modernism were mocked when first performed, exhibited or published.

> That Modernists set out partly to overthrow Romanticism and partly to complete it is explored in *Modernism in Focus*, Lucien Jenkins (Rhinegold 2007).

Romanticism may be complex and contradictory. We may find it hard to pin down when it began and or express precisely what it was about. But its success is demonstrated by the fact that its influence endures to this day.

Romanticism